HOMETOWN TALES
GLASGOW

HOMETOWN TALES is a series of books pairing exciting new voices with some of the most talented and important authors at work today. Each of the writers has contributed an original tale on the theme of hometown, exploring places and communities in the UK where they have lived or think of as home.

Some of the tales are fiction and some are narrative non-fiction – they are all powerful, fascinating and moving, and aim to celebrate regional diversity and explore the meaning of home.

HOMETOWN TALES
GLASGOW

KIRSTY LOGAN
PAUL McQUADE

W&N
WEIDENFELD & NICOLSON

First published in Great Britain in 2018 by Weidenfeld & Nicolson
an imprint of The Orion Publishing Group Ltd
Carmelite House, 50 Victoria Embankment
London EC4Y 0DZ

An Hachette UK Company

1 3 5 7 9 10 8 6 4 2

The Old Asylum in the Woods at the Edge of the Town Where I Grew Up
© Kirsty Logan 2018
A Glasgow Sang © Paul McQuade 2018

A CIP catalogue record for this book is available from the British Library.

ISBN (Hardback) 978 1 4746 0600 4
ISBN (eBook) 978 1 4746 0601 1

Typeset at The Spartan Press Ltd,
Lymington, Hants

Printed and bound in Great Britain by Clays Ltd, St Ives plc

www.orionbooks.co.uk

CONTENTS

The Old Asylum in the Woods at the Edge of the Town Where I Grew Up

Kirsty Logan

KIRSTY LOGAN is the author of the novels *The Gloaming* and *The Gracekeepers*, the short story collections *A Portable Shelter* and *The Rental Heart & Other Fairytales*, and the flash fiction chapbook *The Psychology of Animals Swallowed Alive*. Her books have won the Lambda Literary Award, the Polari First Book Prize, the Saboteur Award, the Scott Prize and the Gavin Wallace Fellowship, and been selected for the Radio 2 Book Club and the Waterstones Book Club. Her short fiction and poetry has been translated into Japanese, Spanish and Italian, recorded for radio and podcasts, exhibited in galleries, and distributed from a vintage Wurlitzer cigarette machine. She lives in Glasgow with her wife.

To everyone who also loved him.

PART ONE

Infinity

1

YOU WEREN'T MEANT to go to the old asylum in the woods at the edge of the town where I grew up. But you could. There was nothing to stop you; no fences or dogs. You could go there to take drugs or get drunk or fuck. You could explore or make a den or hide things. You could get lost among the trees and freeze to death, which one man did.

We went there so I could learn to drive. I was fifteen and thought if I learned now, by the time I was old enough to take my test it would be effortless. I'm now thirty-three and I still can't drive, which isn't the fault of the old asylum or of my dad, who was teaching me. I hated him while he was teaching me to drive, because I hate being bad at things, and I was particularly bad at driving, and I had to hate something so I hated him, because I was a teenager and already hated myself to sufficiency. There were other reasons that I hated him, all of which seemed reasonable at the time and all of which I'm ashamed of now.

We were in a little red Fiat Cinquecento, which was so tiny and janky that if you drove too fast it felt like the bottom of the car was about to fall away under your feet, leaving you pedalling at the ground like the Flintstones. I was never afraid of flying when I was younger, but now I am. I always think the bottom of the plane is going to snap off somehow and fall away from under my feet, even though I know that isn't possible; that planes don't clip together like a Kinder Egg toy. All through my childhood we only ever went on holiday to places you could get to easily by boat, like Denmark or France, because my dad was deathly afraid of flying. So maybe my fear is the fault of my dad. Or the janky Cinquecento. Or maybe it just is.

The part of the old asylum where my dad tried and failed to teach me to drive was an overgrown track in a figure of eight. The track was in a clearing in the woods, about sixty metres by twenty metres – or about sixty-five yards by twenty-two yards, my dad would say, because he was old and still used the imperial system. The track itself was mostly tarmac, grown bumpy and uneven through neglect. The inner teardrops of the figure eight were different sizes. The smaller one held nothing but grass grown to knee-height, and what I remember as an old chicken or rabbit hutch – a wooden box with a mesh front – must be a false memory because there was no reason for something like that to be there.

In the much larger teardrop sat the remains of a building, a Victorian red-brick clock tower with a long, lower building jutting out of one side like the body of a huge dog. The animal image was strengthened by the face of the clock tower, which loomed like a raised head, and the central scooped arch coming down at both ends like legs. When I go to the asylum in my dreams, it's always to that clock tower, even thought I never went inside it in real life. I think other kids did; I'd see empty bottles left around the feet of the building. One story is that it was teenage drinkers having parties and another story is that it was homeless alkies huddling around fires at night and another story, one that I'm positive isn't true, is that it was my dad.

My dad was an alcoholic, though when I was fifteen it was still mostly hidden from me, and I don't know whether this was a conscious decision by my parents or whether I was just too self-absorbed to notice what anyone else was doing. He was a functional alcoholic, in that he only drank in the evenings and was never violent or aggressive, didn't go into work drunk, didn't drive drunk or try to fix things drunk, didn't have any health problems from being drunk – at least not until later when he did several of those things.

A few years later, when it got really bad, my dad climbed up a ladder onto the roof of our house to try to fix something. He had both his arms in slings because he'd fallen off a ladder while drunk – probably the same ladder, and probably he'd been climbing it to try to fix the thing he was now up there again trying to fix. Around and around, over and over, to infinity. He got up to the roof but couldn't get back down, so he called for me and my brother, and we came out into the garden and shouted and pleaded for him to come down, and we were afraid, too afraid to climb the ladder and get him in case he fell and in case we fell with him. Eventually he came down the ladder and we were crying and he was crying and I was so afraid, more afraid than I can tell you, because I'd only seen my dad cry a handful of times in my life and it meant something was very badly wrong. My brother and I put him to bed and told him that we loved him, and I did love him at that moment but I hated him too, I hated him more than I had ever hated anyone. I don't know if I will ever have the capacity to hate someone so much again. I don't see how I could ever be so obsessed and devastated by the inner working of another person's mind. He went to bed and my brother and I went to our rooms and we didn't speak about that night for almost a decade.

But that all came later. At that time my dad drank Tennent's Super in metallic royal blue tins, and once, I got into the car to get a lift to a swimming lesson or the cinema and I found an empty tin rolling around in the backseat footwell and I was afraid then – the starkness of it, the attempt to hide it but not to hide it enough. In my memory I never said anything about it, stayed strong and silent and kept my pain inside, but in reality I know I was a gobby spoiled brat so I probably did say something; I probably went on and on about it, giving everyone metaphorical head-punches until they couldn't hear me any more. I don't think the reason the tin was in the car was that my dad was driving drunk. I think he crept out to the car parked in the street and drank where we wouldn't see him. I think that might have been the beginning of him drinking secretly, which is a ridiculous thing to try to do because everyone knows. After that he went on to white wine, and I don't know much about alcoholism but that doesn't seem like a logical trajectory to me. Wine seems more functional somehow, and I don't know if I think that because people drink it in restaurants, or because my mum drinks it, or because I drink it. He'd drink that secretly too, opening a bottle in the kitchen and pouring it into a wine glass and knocking back the lot in one go. That was another thing I hated him for, another thing the gobby brat of me went on about: why couldn't he just sit in the front room with us and sip a glass of wine like a normal person? We could hear him drinking, could smell him drinking; it wasn't a secret. For years after, the sound of a wine bottle uncorking made me feel sick.

Every childhood is equal parts joy and terror, though sometimes we forget that. I've never understood why anyone would describe the school years as the best of your life. I'd never go back, and I frequently have anxiety dreams that there's a fuck-up with my paperwork and it turns out I don't actually have a Higher Maths or Physics qualification, and in the dream that means I can't be a writer for some reason, and I have to go back and sit the year again as an adult. I wander empty corridors because I've been given a blank class timetable and don't know where I'm supposed to be, or sit in a stuffy hall staring at an exam paper on something I haven't studied.

Nothing particularly terrible happened in my childhood or adolescence, except for the usual stuff with self-harm and getting paralytically drunk and crying so hard you're sick and sexual acts that at the time make you feel upset and dirty and in retrospect were clearly non-consensual but it's too late because you didn't do anything about it at the time and the devastating realisation that your parents are fallible and human and don't have any more answers than you do.

I grew up in Glasgow but I was never afraid of it, even though at the time it was known as the murder capital of Western Europe. There was (and still is) drug addiction and violent crime and poverty and razor gangs, which technically only existed in the 1920s and 30s, though you still occasionally see men with slit scars up their cheeks. They're called Glasgow smiles, or sometimes Cheshire grins after *Alice in Wonderland*'s Cheshire Cat, and this feels like a strange self-absorbed coincidence to me because the only two places I've ever lived are Cheshire and Glasgow.

When I was little and living in Cheshire, I had the usual hardback copy of illustrated fairy tales that children always get for Christmas from some distant but well-meaning relative. Still too young to read the words, I'd spent most of the time looking at the pictures and deciding which flaxen-haired princess was the prettiest. I remember *Rumpelstiltskin* because the picture gave me nightmares. It showed a princess, her wrist bones as tiny and fragile as a bird's, hunched over a spinning wheel. Her head was raised, gazing at a dumpy and gnarled man who was standing on her bed with his muddy feet smearing brown all over her pillows. He looked triumphant, gleeful, stinking. She looked absolutely nothing. My parents hadn't yet read me that story, so my imagination filled in the gaps. I knew it must be a terrible story; what else could have happened to let this desperate young girl invite this dead tree-stump of a man into her bedroom? And what could he have made her agree to, for him to have that look of triumph?

When my dad finally read me the story, it was every bit as horrific as I'd imagined. I was haunted by the desperation of the girl, the feeling of being trapped in a tower with nowhere to go and no one to help her. The knowledge that her own dad had betrayed her. And then that girl had gone on to betray her own daughter, her tiny shrivelled fig of a child, not even conceived of yet and already cursed for ever. Were all girl-children cursed by failure, unable to live up to the expectations their parents set for them, the lies the parents told about them out of greed or desperation? I felt weighted down by the curses of generations of children.

And then I got too busy with the horrible business of being a teenager, and I forgot all about the story and the gnarled triumphant face and the poor unnamed girl trapped in the tower, destined to pass her own horrible fate on to her own child.

See me and my dad driving around and around in our janky car, caught for ever in that place of hate and love and resentment and obsession, me failing to learn and him failing to change. See the track as a figure eight. See it as infinity.

2

MY DAD ALWAYS took my writing seriously. When I was seventeen I printed off, at his request, every single poem and story I'd written in the past few years (there were about sixty of them). He read them all. The poems, needless to say, were absolutely terrible and no one else will ever be forced to read them, whether or not we share blood. My dad put the poems in a suggested order and came up with a title: *Scars*. I was a self-harmer, and I had written about this in several of the poems, and at first I was embarrassed that he'd read them and knew about the self-harm. But he knew perfectly well; my left arm was, and still is, laddered with scars.

I hurt myself in various ways between the ages of thirteen and sixteen, and was hospitalised a couple of times, though I seem to have escaped with only minor scars, for which I am now glad. At the time, I wanted scars. I was proud of them and I didn't hide them. I wanted my pain to show. I know it's a cliché, but it's hard for a teenage girl not to be a cliché.

I read all the books I could find about self-harm; all the novels were patronising shit written by people who had clearly never self-harmed or even wanted to, but some of the non-fiction books were useful. One, called *Bright Red Scream*, told of people whose self-harm was far worse than mine. They were survivors of incest or terrible violence. They carved gouges out of their flesh and pulled out fistfuls of their hair. One girl, I remember, cut off her nipples. Some days I saw that sort of self-destruction as a goal.

My favourite films were all about girls who self-destructed: *The Virgin Suicides; Girl, Interrupted; The Craft.* In the films the girls were always beautiful, their self-destruction beautiful, other people's responses to it beautiful. But deep down I didn't actually want to rip out my hair or cut off my nipples. I wanted to be sad and lovely. I wanted everyone to treat me delicately, like I was special, breakable. I wanted someone to scoop me weeping and bleeding from the shower floor. I wanted to run screaming into the headlights and have someone snatch me out of the way just as the bumper scraped my calves. But I see now that my true self was sturdy and careful. I didn't want something I couldn't come back from. Most of the time I found the book reassuring, because as bad as I got I was never as bad as that. There's a lot of talk about the NHS's failing when it comes to mental health, but I can't complain: in Glasgow in the late '90s, it managed to keep me alive.

During these years I saw several psychologists and I hated them all. I knew what they were going to say before they said it. Or at least I thought I did; I'd read all the books and thought I was terribly clever. In the end I just kept reading books and sorted it out for myself. Perhaps I thought my way out of it, perhaps I grew out of it, perhaps my brain chemistry changed. I don't like to think about that time in any depth, because I don't actually know how or why I made it through, so I'm afraid that I won't be able to repeat the process when I need to. If I start to self-destruct again, I won't know how to come back. I don't know what happened; I just know that one day I felt a bit less awful, then a bit less again, and then after a while I felt almost okay. I don't think mental health is easy and that's no prescription for others, it's just what I did at the time.

But then, I always did think I'd ultimately have to fix myself, because I thought I was cleverer than all the tired grown-ups around me. Perhaps it would have been better if I had needed someone else to help fix me, because it was a terrible lesson to learn: that no one can help you.

I wish my dad hadn't told me I was clever so often when I was growing up. 'Sharp enough to cut yourself,' he said, and how ironically horrible that became. He also said I had 'a brain the size of a planet', like Marvin the Paranoid Android from *The Hitchhiker's Guide to the Galaxy*, and he'd knock out that phrase half-jokingly every time I was doing something he considered insufficiently intellectual like watching MTV or reading Point Horror or lying on the couch doing absolutely nothing, not even daydreaming. I think he'd prefer I read Leonard Cohen poetry and listened to Nick Drake, the way he did as a student; but I was more into Sylvia Plath and riot grrrl and writing my own poetry, all of which was terrible and all of which he read. He'd have read all my books now, including this one, if he hadn't died the year before the first one was published.

3

THE OLD ASYLUM was called Woodilee, and it lives
still in my imagination as vivid and timeless and ex-
plorable as Narnia, Hogwarts, Middle Earth. Around
the old building and the infinity symbol were woods,
which weren't particularly big or dark or looming,
not like fairy-tale woods, no wolves or bears, perhaps
a fox and some squirrels at a push. There was a cat
though, a little ginger slinking thing that my dad and
I saw when I was driving circles in first gear in the
janky Cinquecento, and I panicked because I didn't
want to hit the cat, even though it was off to the side
and unlikely to sprint in front of the car, which in any
case was going at a crawl, bumping over grassy hum-
mocks and rents in the tarmac, all of which I became
immediately convinced were cats.

All my childhood, we had cats. When I was born,
my parents already had a cat, a practice baby, a

grumpy stripy ginger called Biggles after the adventure novels my dad used to read as a boy. My childhood was spent making Biggles look at the pictures I'd drawn, taking photos of Biggles sleeping in the bed I'd made him out of Lego and an old silk cushion, tapping my fingertip on Biggles' little pink nose until he got annoyed and hissed at me. Originally Biggles had a sister called Cleo who my parents said ran away to live with an old lady up the road, but I realise now she must have been hit by a car. When Biggles got old, my best friend's cat had kittens – one of them died during the birth, or perhaps just before or just after, and the mother cat left it at the top of the stairs, this thumb-sized slimy thing with tiny slits for eyes, and I was so afraid of it that I couldn't even tell anyone I was afraid.

Six of the kittens lived, and we took two of them and called them Amber and Tigger. When I was twelve we moved to Glasgow from Cheshire and took the cats with us, loose in the car the whole journey: Amber crouched and wary on the parcel shelf, Tigger perched on my lap with his claws flexing happily into the flesh of my thigh. We all lived together in the new house for the next decade – my dad, my mum, my brother, me, the two cats. When my parents separated, my dad took both the cats. In all of those years, Amber never stopped being restless and flighty, twitching at loud noises. Not long after my dad moved into his new house alone, Amber disappeared, and at first my dad told me she'd run away to live with an old lady, but later he either forgot he'd told me that or realised I was twenty-two and had lost several friends and three out of four grandparents and so was used to the idea of death, and told me she'd probably been hit by a car.

After my dad died I took Tigger to the first-floor tenement flat where I lived with my girlfriend. Tigger was old and content and mostly just lay on the rug in front of the fire waiting for someone to scratch his fat furry tummy. He still had a tiny pretty face and huge eyes, like a kitten, so it was easy to forget how old he was. That flat had no garden and it was on a main road so Tigger had to get used to a litter tray, which was fine except we noticed almost immediately that there was blood in his urine. Possibly there had been for years, but he pissed in the garden so no one noticed. I spent hundreds of pounds on vet fees to try to make that cat live longer. Actually I don't know if I wanted him to live longer, or I just couldn't stand to think that he was in pain and I hadn't done anything about it. He had scans and blood tests and pills and more pills and yet more pills, crushed up with a spoon every morning and stirred into his Whiskas. By the end his meow sounded like Winston Churchill and he had lumps on his back and he swayed when he ran and his hind legs hurt so much you couldn't pick him up. He couldn't clean his back end so every fortnight we'd have to bath him to wash off the caked-on shit and bits of litter, which Tigger hated, though he never struggled or scratched, just stood there in the lukewarm water gazing up at me with an expression like I had profoundly and shockingly betrayed him.

I kept him alive far longer than I should. I hate thinking about it now. But I just couldn't let him go. My dad had looked after him for years, out of love or duty or to show the world that he could take care of something even if he couldn't take care of himself. I wanted to show him that I could do it too. I knew love and duty. I never felt like an adult until my dad died, and then every wall felt flimsy and temporary, like stage dressing that was about to collapse, when before everything felt trustworthy, ancient, anchored. But he was gone and I had to be an adult now, and part of being an adult is taking care of both yourself and something other than yourself.

I took our cat to the vet and got him put to sleep. I watched as he took his last breath, his lungs filling and then not, just like my dad's had done when I watched him die.

I SPENT MOST of the late '90s and early 2000s listening to music. Mostly I listened to chart hip-hop, pop and rock, the sort of stuff that got played on the radio or covered in magazines like *Rock Sound* and *NME*. *Rock Sound* launched the year I turned fifteen, and was my favourite music magazine because it came with a free compilation CD in every issue; I'd listen to it right the way through with intense concentration, as if I was going to be tested on it later, making biro dashes against the songs I liked so I could save up and buy the CDs at HMV.

The problem came when I got into riot grrrl – which began with Hole's *Live Through This*, an album I still adore, and expanded to Sleater-Kinney's *The Hot Rock*, L7's *Bricks Are Heavy*, Babes in Toyland's *Painkillers*, Bikini Kill's *Pussy Whipped* (ten years after this, aged twenty-five, I would get one of my

25

first paid short story publications with 'Rebel Girl', a lesbian erotica story inspired by track ten of this album), Team Dresch's *Personal Best*, and albums by other female-led rock bands like Rasputina's *How We Quit the Forest*, My Ruin's *Speak and Destroy*, Jack Off Jill's *Clear Hearts Grey Flowers*, and The Distillers' *Sing Sing Death House*. Most of those CDs were only available on import – you couldn't even get them in the four-storey Tower Records next to the main train station in Glasgow, which is now an abandoned building covered in gig posters and pigeon shit. The CDs had to be ordered online, and that involved a lot of effort as I had to convince my dad that the CDs were absolutely necessary to my survival and sanity as a human being, and so could he please order them on his credit card please please oh please and maybe there would be customs and postage from overseas but I needed them I really really needed them please. Three weeks later, the CDs arrived in a mysterious white cardboard package covered in interesting foreign stickers. I kept the empty packages for years, not quite sure what I wanted to do with them but sure that they should not just be disposed of like old crisp packets. These packages were special; they were a part of my emotional and intellectual upbringing. In a few years when I was a famous musician-writer-artist-designer, people would want these objects. They would want to know where I came from, and where I came from was those sticker-encrusted packages.

I listened to each new CD on repeat for days at a time. I pored over the lyrics booklet, reading the words through, savouring every line like poetry. Because they were poetry, more so than what we read at school, those dusty clunking words by dry rustling men about starting wars and winning wars and losing wars, and loving unattainable women and gaining attainable women, and men doing all that dull shit that men have spent history doing. I wanted life and blood and the words left at the bottom of lungs when everything else had been screamed out. I wanted to hear what it felt for a girl like me to love a girl like me. I wanted to know how to be strong and how to fail and how to pick myself up again. I wanted to know that I wasn't the only one. I wanted to know what girls had to say and I wanted to join in when they said it. I wanted them. I wanted everything about them: their shoes, their hair, their polka-dot vintage dresses, their plastic barrettes, their thoughts, their heartbreaks, their desires, their being-desireds, their sympathies, their company, their empty lipsticked glasses, their lungs, their tongues. And the closest I could get to that came packaged in little white boxes covered in stickers and went straight from the little shiny disc through my chunky fist-sized headphones and into the curlicues of my brain, full of empty spaces like the alveoli of lungs, ready to be filled with the air of girls telling the truth to girls.

I wouldn't be a writer today if not for that music and everything it taught me.

My dad tried to get into my music. Once, in the car, I put on the soundtrack to *Scream 3*, which was crammed full of the worst of early-2000s pop-metal like Slipknot, System of a Down, Sevendust, Static-X, Staind and some other bands that didn't begin with S but were also shit. The first track was 'What If' by Creed, which I'm listening to on Spotify as I write this paragraph, and – I'll just say I appreciate even more that my dad let me play it in the car. But he tried, just like he always tried to connect with me, and as we waited at a red light and I pressed play on the CD, he swung the volume knob right round, louder even than I could handle, although I spent half my life arguing with my mum because I played my music too loud. But I grinned at him and pretended I liked it, just like he pretended he liked it, and we sat at the light with our eardrums throbbing, the music too loud to talk over. Then the next track started: Slipknot, a band I never liked, even though all my friends liked them so I used to mosh to 'Wait and Bleed' during Unders Night at the Cathouse, where we had to get drunk on peach schnapps at each other's houses before we went into town because you couldn't buy drinks inside and if you tried to smuggle in a bottle of cheap vodka they'd always know and take it off you, even if it was in your bra or at your hip, held sweaty to your skin by the side of your pants. I also went to see them play live at the Barrowlands, which was a tame and boring gig, even though I read several reviews which mentioned the drummer setting his kit on fire and hitting his head so hard he passed out, both of which I somehow missed even though I was in the room at the time. When Slipknot started, I slid the volume back down. But I still remember it because my dad was trying. We both tried, but he tried harder.

My early childhood nights had their own music. Weekday nights were the low murmur of the television and the high-low slow-dance of my parents' speech; or the clatter of dishes and cutlery overlaid with my mum's soft humming; or the muffled bass thump and sweeping violins from the stereo – those times, I imagined my parents dancing together, twirling around on the living room carpet and dipping to a kiss.

Weekend nights were the raucous laughter of a dozen adults rising from the dining room underneath my bedroom, where my parents had dinner parties and ate oatcakes and cheese and olives and capers and other nasty things, and drank gin and wine and whisky and other even nastier things. They played Trivial Pursuit and my dad shouted that the answer on the card must be wrong because there was no way he could possibly be wrong, that was definitely not how you spelled fluorescent and that was definitely not the date of the Great Fire of London and that was definitely not the right publication order of Hermann Hesse's books, and my mum would laugh and tell him he could win all the cheeses that he wanted, no one cared, and I found that strange because the cheese they ate was horrible – it smelled like feet and it was squishy and had blue bits in it – so why would anyone argue over it?

I slid out of bed and tiptoed one step at a time downstairs, jumping over the creaky bottom step, and pushed open the dining room door. The faces of the grown-ups glowed soft and young in the candlelight, but none as much as my mum – her skin was the most perfect, her eyes the brightest, her earrings the prettiest. She threw back her head and laughed, and I was sure that everyone in the room must be transfixed by the beauty of her exposed throat.

Candlelight flickered along my dad's wall of books, of which he'd said I could read any I wanted, so I went straight for Stephen King's *Carrie* and J.G. Ballard's *Crash*, one because it had blood on the cover and one because it had an exposed breast, both of which scared me and were signs that I definitely should not be reading those books, and after the first page I realised that not only were they books I shouldn't read, they were books I couldn't read. Instead I read George Orwell's *Animal Farm*, which was about animals so surely couldn't be miles away from *The Wind in the Willows* or Colin Dann books I loved. I finished the book despite the fact I barely understood a word. A few years later, when I was a bit older but still too young, I read *Carrie* and *Crash*, and I did understand them, although a part of me wishes I hadn't; that I could have stayed a little longer in the dream of childhood before waking up.

Once, when my parents were having a dinner party, or a Trivial Pursuit and gin party if you prefer, they forgot I hadn't been put to bed and I stayed up late in the front room to watch a film on Channel 4 called *Bandit Queen*, a biopic about Phoolan Devi, who was married off as a child, only to escape, be gang-raped, become the leader of a group of bandits, surrender to police, be imprisoned, and later be released. The gang-rape scene, where Devi is stripped, beaten, and sent to fetch water from the well in full view of everyone in the village, none of whom help her, haunted me. It haunts me still. It was the first time I realised that such cruelty existed in the world. That film was too old for me, but I'm glad I saw it, and I'm glad it scared and upset me. I had a safe and happy childhood, and that film taught me things that I would eventually need to learn. I was afraid, but I was safe, and I think that's the kindest way to learn anything.

My dad was on his feet trying to act something out to the amusement of the other grown-ups. The table held a Trivial Pursuit board, scattered question cards, little coloured triangles and the round thing the triangles went in. There were pistachio shells, olive pits with the dull flesh clinging in strips, a haphazard tower block of cheeses: grown-up food. The room smelled of strangers' perfume, candle wax and gin.

I tiptoed in, unnoticed by the adults. Suddenly my mum cried out my name – that beautiful rolled 'r' in the middle, how she dropped her tongue and let the word fill her mouth, instead of pushing it into the roof and flattening it, making the rolled 'r' an 'ugh' the way that everyone else we knew in Cheshire did. She scolded me for being out of bed so far past bedtime, then swept me up into her lap. I watched the chaos at the end of the dinner party like the final scene of a film. Within five minutes I was asleep, and the sounds of the dinner party seeped into my dreams. When I woke I was back in my bed, the dining table cleared, the candles in the drawer, all evidence gone like it was a fairy party and they'd all disappeared back underground.

Once, I crept downstairs on a weekday night to find my dad alone in the front room, wearing a pair of big yellow headphones, bopping around the room in total silence. He scooped me up and I rested my head on his shoulder where I could hear the music; the song was 'Killer' by Adamski and Seal. He held me like that, both of us listening to the beat through opposite sides of the headphone, and he swayed around the room with me, my extra weight adding more spin when he turned, my bare feet dangling, his hands locked under me, and I don't remember ever feeling so safe.

5

IN 1999, WHEN my dad and I were doing our driving lessons, you couldn't get sectioned to Woodilee. It was almost completely closed by then; only a few small buildings by the entrance remained open, rebuilt as modern boxes, not the gothic red-brick glories my dad and I drove our slow circles around. Back in the days when people were put into Woodilee, when mental health facilities were still called asylums, I don't think sectioning existed. The Mental Health Act 1983, which came into law the year before I was born, means that you can be involuntarily detained in hospital if your mental health makes you a danger to yourself or others. If I'd lived in that town in 1899 instead of 1999, carving lines in my arm and refusing to eat and taking overdoses and crying every day and telling my parents I was bisexual, I'm sure I would have been put in Woodilee. I loved the thought of being sectioned. I loved the thought of losing control; of giving control over to someone else, an adult who knew what they were doing.

I don't know what sort of people stayed at Wood-ilee at the time we went driving there. I think maybe it was a care home for old people. Or for people of any age who couldn't look after themselves. All I know is that people stayed there, and they weren't locked in because they didn't need to be locked in. One time, a guy wandered out of the front door and into the woods around the buildings. It was autumn, not cold but not warm either, and he was out there in the woods for a few days before his body was found, frozen to death. I don't know why he wasn't found sooner; the woods weren't large. It's easy to be lost if you want to be.

My dad would occasionally talk about suicide. He said that if it ever got too much for him, he'd go into the woods and take off all his clothes and wait to freeze to death. He said it would be a good way to go. He said it matter-of-factly, wryly almost. I had read somewhere that if people talk about suicide then they're probably not going to actually do it, and also I thought if he could talk about it so wryly then he couldn't really

36

mean it. He also once told me that the best way to kill yourself (or someone else) is an overdose of insulin, because you just slip into a coma and die quickly and painlessly. If you want it to go unnoticed you can inject the person between their toes or under their tongue. At the time it didn't seem strange that he was telling me this; he told me lots of things, anything I asked about.

As a teenager I used to borrow non-fiction books from the library and make notes from them in a little notebook, for no apparent reason. It wasn't for school or a project; it was just because I was interested, and I loved the book, and I wanted to keep a bit of it for myself. Once, I spent a weekend transcribing my audiotape of Roald Dahl's *The Witches*. I already had the novel, but this wasn't the reading of the novel, it was a dramatisation, so I laid it all out like I thought an audio script should look. It took hours and hours, particularly because my tape player was on the other side of the room from the computer, so I had to keep getting up and running across the room to switch off the tape, then running back to quickly type as much of the dialogue as I could remember. I'm often asked when I first knew I wanted to be a writer, and for some reason I've never told that story, though as I write it now I see it serves as an adorably nerdy origin story.

One afternoon I was lying on my bed taking notes from a book about superstitions from all over the world (why? I just was; teenagers are weird), and I read a word I didn't understand. My dad was at the computer, which was in my bedroom, so I asked him: 'Dad, what does phallic mean?' A pause, and he said, 'It means shaped like a penis.' Luckily he had his back to me because I immediately died of embarrassment. I hope you get to live your whole life without hearing either of your parents say *penis*.

When I was much younger, instead of bedtime stories my dad would do Question Time, which I can only assume he named after a political debate show for his own amusement. I was five, so all I knew was that Question Time was when I had my dad to myself – a rarer occurrence since my little brother had been born the previous year. I have a photo of when my brother first came home from the hospital, and my dad is holding us both, my brother an enormous red slug-baby born three weeks overdue and me a serious and Victorian-looking four-year-old dressed in a nightie and holding a toy seal, and my dad is the happiest I can ever remember seeing him; he's beaming so wide it looks like his face is about to split into sunlight. During Question Time, my dad would lie on the edge of my single bed – pink frilly duvet cover and sheets, as I was still in the phase where I refused to wear or sleep under or put in my hair anything that wasn't pink – and he'd answer my questions. I was obsessed with the milkman, and asked my dad over and over how the milk got into the bottles for the man to deliver in the mornings. I asked him how fish got into the sea, how cars go, what ghosts were really, why Gran powdered her nose but Mum didn't, why some people didn't have food, what I was like when I was a baby, what I'd be like when I grew up. He always knew the answers, though I realise now he must have made up a large portion of them, because he was thirty-six at the time and that's the age my wife is now and she knows the answers to a lot of questions but she doesn't know half the shit I asked my dad when I was five.

I kept asking him questions all through my life and he always answered them. As I got older, the questions were less fanciful, more practical. How do I pay my council tax? Can I return these jeans even though I took the labels off, if they ripped the first time I wore them? How should I format my CV? Is it better to have the same supplier for your gas and electric or shop around? He always knew.

After he died I had so many questions. What were we supposed to do? How did we cancel his mobile phone contract? Where was his will? Which was his favourite jumper, so that I could keep it? Which coffin should we choose: the cheaper, environmentally friendly cardboard one or the traditional, fancy, chunky, expensive one; and since he was being cremated anyway did it matter less or more, as the coffin would presumably be burned with him and mixed with his ashes forever? The only person who always knew the answer to my questions was my dad. Several times I reached for my phone to call him before remembering. I knew he was dead, but also he couldn't be dead. In that moment before reality came back into focus, there were two of him: the dead dad who I had to deal with, and the permanent dad who would always help me.

I kept obsessive journals between the ages of fourteen and twenty-two, and now when I put them in date order I see them change as I aged: from stolen school jotters to little flimsy floral things to solid A4 lumps papered with magazine cutouts to plain A5 hardbacks in solid colours. I remember writing in my journal, age fifteen, around when my dad started talking about going into the woods: *'If he dies, I will die. My heart will just stop beating.'*

Just the thought of my dad dying made my heart stutter. But surely he couldn't die. He was my dad, for fuck's sake. Dads don't die.

After he died, when I was twenty-seven, I didn't die. My heart didn't stop. If I'm honest, it barely stuttered. I'd spent so many years imagining his death that when it finally came, it was ... not a relief, but not a surprise either.

I have a handful of terrible memories of my dad, and thousands of good ones. But the one I keep coming back to is neither good nor terrible. It's us at the old asylum, driving infinity loops as a man was dying alone in the woods, just the way my dad said he wanted to die.

PART TWO

Mythology

I'VE TRIED TO write about... the past decade...

1

I'VE TRIED TO write about Woodilee four times in the past decade. I've written a novel set there, and then I've rewritten that novel three times, each time making it slightly less terrible, but still nowhere near good enough to be an actual novel. None of them really ended; I thought, in my memory, that I had ended them, but now I look back over the files I see that I got to a point and just stopped writing. I never reached any conclusions.

2

EWAN WORKED AT Woodilee in the early 1970s as part of his medical degree.

Ewan was in his early twenties, and his first child was still ten years away from being conceived.

Ewan was six feet tall and had arms as thick as pythons.

Ewan could do long division in his head.

Ewan had perfect pitch, could throw a rugby ball accurately with his eyes closed, and could have been a punk rock superstar.

Ewan had already read every book by Hermann Hesse, Graham Greene, Aldous Huxley and Yukio Mishima.

Ewan was tall and handsome and his skin was tanned gold.

Ewan could sail and ski and swim the whole length of the swimming pool underwater.

Ewan had a lot of girlfriends, and he wrote notes in his Leonard Cohen and T.S. Eliot books, dedicating poems and individual lines to different girls.

Ewan woke at dawn every morning and did push-ups while composing sonatas in his head.

Ewan breakfasted on fresh fruit and home-made porridge.

Ewan walked to work, the summer air warming the dawn goosebumps from his arms. When Ewan was young, it was always summer.

Ewan said: 'Good morning.'

Ewan heard 'Good morning' back from everyone he met, and every single one of them smiled, and every single one thought about what a wonderful man he was.

Ewan spent his days picking up the things that the residents of Woodilee threw to the floor.

Ewan asked them polite questions and calmly answered their screams and weeping.

Ewan always lifted his feet properly when he walked.

Ewan thought, sometimes in passing, that the people he looked after were awful and irritating and a drain on society.

Ewan thought he would rather be a banker, or a lawyer, or a doctor.

Ewan would be impatient and bored.

Ewan would hate.

Ewan knew these thoughts would not stick; they flowed through his mind like soapslick.

Ewan picked up his feet and rubbed the frown from between his eyebrows. Back then, the frown was not chiselled in.

Ewan worked at Woodilee for a while, and then he left.

Perhaps it was as simple as that for him. Perhaps he forgot all about it; perhaps it didn't haunt him, not then and not later, even though he'd grown up in a house two minutes, as the crow flies, from the old asylum. He didn't think he'd go back to Woodilee decades later, with his bleeding, itching, acne-spattered teenage daughter in a janky red Cinquecento. He would not have imagined the possibility of that, just as he wouldn't have wondered at the possibility of coming back as a patient.

3

'I FOUND YOUR webpage a week or so ago through a thicket of web browsing.

I can't remember how I found your page, maybe wanting to read something new – something Scottish?

Or maybe you are a facebook friend of a friend of a friend of my niece or nephew, I don't really recall how I landed on your site.

I read some of your work and am impressed with your earthy, honest voice. I wondered if you might be a Logan I knew.

So I went facebooking and twittering and found the picture of your Dad on the bike in Nigeria.

So I knew you were – I'd seen that picture over forty years ago.

'My name is David and I went to school with your Dad.

I left Glasgow and went to Art School in London. I came to the US for a Graduate Degree and have lived here ever since.

I feel like I am getting back in touch with my roots. I also have been in touch with friends I had not seen for years. I did hope I might get in touch with your Dad this winter.

I was unprepared for your announcement of Ewan's illness and sudden death.

It seemed that I had found him again only to lose him. I am very sorry for your loss, he died too young.

I heard bits and pieces of news about him and your family over the years.

'I only knew Ewan well for a few formative years. We were unalike – Ewan was athletic, outgoing, clever.

I was decidedly unathletic, asthmatic, shy, artsy, but we did both share a sarcastic sense of humour.

He was popular and handsome and I felt so lucky to be in his circle of friends.

We lived on the other side of town from each other. The footbridge over the train tracks became the small secret door into the enchanted garden for me.

I can still recall the frisson in my footsteps on the

bridge. I loved your family, Ewan's parents seemed more glamorous than mine (don't other people's relatives always seem that way?). They had travelled and lived abroad. When the boys came to school they had quite pronounced Lancashire accents, they quickly lost it. But it did make them seem more exotic. We would play tennis and go swimming together, he moved so easily and gracefully it was a pleasure to watch him run.

Towards 6th year at school I started dropping out and we drifted apart – I started hanging out with an arts group and we published a poetry magazine. Ewan contributed several poems, and that was the last real contact I had with him.

It was not a long time knowing him, but I'll always remember him so young, so beautiful, so alive.'

About a year after Ewan died, I received an email from a man he knew at school when they were both boys. Or men, or something in-between. It's strange enough to know our parents had sex – our existence is the evidence, after all. Stranger still to be confronted by a man who had clearly fancied my recently dead dad.

What was so fascinating to me about this email

was to see how David had mythologised Ewan, made him into a golden statue, gleaming in his memory, much as I had. I wish that David could have known Ewan later – when his hands shook from Parkinson's, when his eyebrows flaked white, when he wore a track in the carpet between his bed and his couch and his back door, where he stood smoking into the suburban night. I loved him then, but I knew that other people's love wasn't unconditional. I liked that David never knew Ewan like that. He only knew him as the athletic golden boy of the town, and his house as a portal to exotic adventures. It's not a fiction, though it's a story I never knew existed. How many stories are out there, true as memory, solid as dreams, waiting to be spoken?

I think that was the first time I realised that I was not the only one who had a story about Ewan. I was so caught up in my own grief – as self-absorbed and brattish as ever – that it didn't even occur to me that others had lost someone when Ewan died. My grandfather had lost a son. My uncles had lost a brother. My brother had lost his dad. My mum – perhaps this was the most complex of all, because what had she lost? Not a husband; and not an ex-husband, as they had never divorced, only separated. She was a widow, and not a widow. She – like everyone else who had ever met him – has stories about Ewan that I'll never know; their own mythologies.

Ewan's family – my family – is easy to mythologise. They're structured like a fairy tale. The strong, silent father. The patrician matriarch. The three boys, each so different, like the brothers in a story about to go out and seek their fortune. As soon as they were old enough, they scattered from Glasgow to Cumbria, Cheshire and North London. My grandmother had specific plans for each of her three boys. There was the eldest, who was going to be a politician but instead became a Buddhist carpenter in Brooklyn, married to an Indian-American poet. The middle, who was going to be a doctor but instead became a medical rep and suburban father of two before dying suddenly at fifty-eight. The youngest, who was going to be a lawyer and then was a lawyer, before switching to something inexplicable in finance, and settling into family life in London with the kind of money I've never otherwise seen in real life.

I look at the photos now and I can't understand that this is my family, and not people from a film. If the woman in the photos didn't have my grandmother's unmistakable Roman nose, I'd suspect they were nothing more than beautiful strangers, the photos that come in the frames when you buy them. Their life is a part of mine, mere decades away, but it feels like another world.

My favourites – the most make-believe-feeling ones – are of when they lived in Nigeria in the 1950s. My grandfather worked for the government doing something mysterious that I still don't understand, though I knew that they once hosted the Queen for tea. The photos are sheened with nostalgia, fake-old, like they've gone through an Instagram filter. They look posed, too beautiful. The three boys piled onto the back of a bicycle, all chubby limbs and golden hair. The boys again – always three, the fairy-tale brothers arranged by height – pushing a car stuck at the grassy side of a road. My grandmother leaning sassily against a boxy vintage American car, which of course wasn't vintage at the time, wearing an hourglass floral-print frock which I wish I owned; now it would be classic vintage, hundreds of pounds in a boutique. The Logans never bought vintage, or second-hand as it was called then; everything new and everything good quality, so much so that when my grandfather died just before I bought my first flat,

I could fill it with their 1970s Ercol furniture, and a couch that was older than me but still in better condition than anything I could afford.

For years I've been planning a story about my family, who I don't think of as 'my family' but as 'the Logans'. It will be a rambling, glorious, myth-sticky story where nothing feels quite real but everything is confession. It will be the tale of three brothers: one who climbs up into the sky, one who climbs over into bodies, one who climbs down into the earth. But it will really be the story of a woman, and how the world won't let her be the thing she wants to be, never mind the three things she wants to be, so she makes boys and lives through them instead.

After someone dies, it's easy to make them into a story. Living people are messy and won't fit between pages; they have traceable beginnings, but their middles are uneven and their endings unknowable. You can make a dead person be whoever you want them to. Facts are porous and flexible, and every story has more sides than people involved. Who's left to argue with you now? If they didn't write it down, the only truth is yours.

4

WOODILEE HAS ALWAYS been a place for hauntings. Ghosts sleep in the veins of the leaves on the trees and in between the bricks of the old abandoned buildings. They wind their way through the branches and scatter the birds from their nests at the tops of the tallest branches. Ghosts whisper and shout and plead and profess love and hate. They cannot be stopped and they cannot be silenced.

Woodilee has always been a place for the dregs. Perhaps in later times, the residents would have been diagnosed as schizophrenic, or overworked, or depressed, or developmentally disabled, or anxious, or homosexual, or promiscuous, or a little too willing to question religion. They could not or would not act in the way that they were told. Woodilee would set them right. So they were tucked neatly away behind the barred windows, given daily pills, set to playing nice games on the flawless lawn, and told to be quiet. And they were quiet, until they died quietly, and were quietly buried. Woodilee worked perfectly.

Then times changed, and times decided that Woodilee was not working. It ceased its function as a mental hospital. The vast arched corridors, the overgrown gardens, the ransacked medicine cabinets, the wrought-iron bed frames, the stained and torn mattresses, the winding basement corridors with locked doors that no one had the keys to unlock, the twisted clock tower that was always running late no matter how often it was reset, the uneven stairwells, the patients' common room with the doctors' office as a panopticon: everything left to rot and ruin. A few small buildings near Woodilee's main entrance were rebuilt, made wheelchair-friendly and forced to conform to new safety standards. These buildings were the perfect size for the three members of live-in staff, a common room for six further members of day staff, a janitorial cupboard, a waiting room and reception area, a kitchen and dining room, and most important of all: bedrooms for two dozen elderly residents. Woodilee had been reborn as a care home.

No longer could they enjoy the flat emerald lawns and the games to be played on them, the mysteries of winding basement corridors, or the easily picked lock on the medicine cabinet. But the ghosts had not gone anywhere. They had lain quiet for a long time, but they were still there, sleeping in the mortar between the bricks of the buildings, at the top of the tallest trees, behind the face of the clock in the tower, deep underneath the soil: in the very veins of Woodilee.

It's night and I'm in the woods. In the middle of the clearing is a building, three storeys high. At the top of the building is a clock tower, both of the clock's hands raised to midnight. Or midday, though it doesn't matter as it's wrong either way. Closer to the building, I run my free hand along the stonework. It feels rough and oddly soft, spongy and warm from the layer of moss. The stairway leads to a walkway, a stone corridor with no glass in its windows. I want to climb the stairs, but I fear the floor crumbling out from under me.

I hear the ghosts all around – disguised as birds singing their thoughts and the rustle of trees, but I know it's ghosts, whispering secrets.

I climb the stairs, keeping close to the edges in case the middle collapses. Upstairs in the stone corridor,

I can see further across the grounds. All that lies in front of me is miles and miles of trees and dead leaves. The woods are endless, timeless. The sky has faded: hot orange to dark red streaked with cancerous black. Night calls.

I step across the clusters of dead leaves and piles of bird feathers, making sure not to trip on broken masonry. As dark falls on Woodilee, I listen. The ghosts still call, but I block them out. All of them, except for my dad. I run my fingers along the rough bare stone. I feel the dust and grit of years in my fingerprints. I feel tiny burrs breaking my skin, entering my body.

I think of my dad – his youth, his dreams; his illness, his shaking hands. I think of the way that he did his crosswords in pen and the trust of his strong hands lifting my toddler body to the sky, the trust I found in his grasp. I remember his wall of books, the spines I memorised. I remember his stubbled jaw, the white peppered rasp of it. I remember how he looked after me in a way that I would never have the patience or selflessness to look after him, even at his sickest. I remember who he used to be, and who he had dreamed of being, and who he became. I think of how he loved me and how I loved him. I think of all the things I wanted to say to him, and how I can't now, and how I don't need to anyway because he already knew.

I think of how we tried.

5

IF WOODILEE HAD not been largely abandoned by 1999, if it still served its old functions, if people could still be shut up in it and forgotten, if all of these things – then Ewan would have been there. Perhaps he would be there still.

Ewan would be a patient, not an employee.
Ewan would not get up at dawn and do three dozen sit-ups.
Ewan would not get paid to answer weeping questions.
Ewan would not pick up his feet.

Ewan would wear clothes that did not fit him and let his hair grease flat to his scalp.
Ewan would not focus his eyes.
Ewan would stop wearing his glasses – no need;

nothing he needed to look at – and the dents on the side of his nose would eventually smooth out.

Ewan would forget how to do long division in his head.

Ewan would stare at a bee buffeting against the half-open window for minutes, and hours, and days.

Ewan would let his medication swallow him.

Ewan would sink into chemical bliss, right to the black bottom, the water warm and clear.

Ewan would blink, and he would smile.

Ewan would have no children.

Ewan would write nothing and read nothing.

Ewan would not be sad.

PART THREE

Honesty

1

I'VE TRIED TO make my dad into a story. I've tried to make Woodilee into a story. But both are too big and too messy and too strange to me. I never properly knew them when they existed, and I have no hope of knowing them now that they're gone.

When someone is gone, all you want is more time with them. To say something or hear something or just be with them. You make a deal with the universe: I'll be good for the rest of my life if I can have another day with them. I'll give everything. Anything. For less than a day. A minute. A second. A single glance, a word.

But it doesn't matter whether you ask for ten years or ten seconds, because you can't have it.

I'm now two years older than my dad was when I was born. I don't have any children. I don't want to die without passing on something of my dad. The Logans are dying out. My brother and I are the only two Logans left who might have children, and my brother does not want any. My two uncles and I are the only living people with the exact Logan-blue eyes of my dad and my grandpa. One of my strongest memories is sitting at the dinner table at my grand-parents' house – the dinner table I now own – and looking at that row of blue eyes and feeling like I was a part of something. I want to pass that on. If I pass on anything, I want it to be that. But I know I don't get to choose.

I think a lot about heritage, particularly in the last few years. It's impossible to avoid, even if I wasn't prone to story-making. My wife and I want children, and I worry about what I'll give to the ones I birth. I think of *Rumpelstiltskin*, and how afraid I was of the pictures in my fairy-tale book, and how the reality of the story was even worse than I could imagine. I think of the girl who was betrayed by her father and went on to betray her own daughter, her tiny shrivelled fig of a child, not even conceived of yet and already cursed for ever.

On my bad days I think that I have nothing good

to pass on; that I'm nothing but a leering crinkled goblin-thing, clumsy and scarred, my mouth an awful cavern of wonky teeth and rotten words, my flesh sagging lazy, my brain stuttering and cavernous. I'm the worst possible combination of my parents; a magnification of their bad and an absence of their good. On my better days I think that my DNA is worth something, that I'm proud of what I was given and what I have made with it.

I worry about what I might pass on to a child, but I know that my genetics are no better and no worse than any other potential parent's. A child is not a clone; a child is a collaboration, a brand new thing, greater than the sum of its parts. Our child will share my biology, but it will have another biological parent too. And more importantly than that, any child my wife and I have, we will raise together.

My dad and I had a lot in common: those blue eyes, a love of the sea, a tendency to the dramatic, an acknowledgement that only a few things keep us from leaping off the edge of the cliff, that slow forever dive. There was a time I was fit for the asylum and so was my dad. The long shadow of Woodilee will always lie over my history. Do I really want to pass that on?

But my dad passed it on to me, and I learned from him. Maybe the sickness gets a little better each time. Maybe it's not an infinity symbol.

2

AFTER MY PARENTS split up, my dad moved into a new house. The upstairs bedroom had belonged to the daughter of the previous homeowners, and that became my room when I stayed over, which I didn't like to do very often because my dad's house was always stuffy-hot and chilly at the same time, and the hall carpet smelled like cat pee no matter how many times it was cleaned, and there was nothing I wanted to eat in the fridge, and my dad drank secretly and annoyingly in the kitchen. I preferred to meet him in town or the Southside for lunch, and there were only three different places that we went to over and over, because it was hard to find somewhere that he could park right outside and not have to go up any stairs at all, because he walked with a stick and was very unsteady. He always paid for lunch, no matter how many times I tried to, though he let me leave the tip.

At my dad's house I filled two Ikea bookcases with the books I didn't need enough to take to my mum's but didn't want to give away. The books at my mum's were the person I was now; the books at my dad's were previous versions of me, and staying at his was an opportunity to wander through my past. I slid my finger along the spines of the prepublication proof of Jacqueline Wilson's *Girls in Love* I'd got from my bookseller mum and had been so obsessed with that I'd traced the illustrated lists from the book and made my own; the crack-spined Robin Hobb paperbacks I'd stolen from my high school boyfriend only to realise I didn't fancy him as much as I fancied Burrich from the Farseer Trilogy; the old copy of J.R.R. Tolkien's *The Hobbit* that I'd struggled through even though I hated it because I'd loved the story of my dad calling in fake-sick to school for a week so he could lie in bed and read the whole *Lord of the Rings* trilogy. I always preferred the stories of my dad – the mythology of him, the knowable character, the neatness – to the conflicting, messy reality.

My dad paid a couple he knew to come and sort the house and garden for a few hours a week, so the carpet was always vacuumed, the bathroom bleachy, the small lawn mown. But when my mum and brother and I went into the house after he died to clean it up to sell, we found that a vine from the garden had worked its way between the window frame and the pane. It was so strong that we couldn't pull it out. I had to get secateurs from the garage; they were so rusty they would barely cut, and I ended up hacking and sawing at the vine to try to wrench it free. I don't mind the sight of blood but I can't look at the needle when I give blood; I get queasy at the memory of having in a drip or an IV shunt. I've always been disgusted by the thought of something that's half inside and half outside of my body, something that isn't a part of me but isn't safely not-me either, and those vines gave me the same feeling of revulsion.

At the age of twenty-three, the year after I finished uni, I had a tonsillectomy. It's not a serious operation but it does involve a general anaesthetic, an overnight hospital stay, and the danger of a tonsil bleed. Every night before the operation, I dreamt of waking with my throat clogged with blood; of choking on blood; of coughing up huge gushing spatters of blood on white walls; of dying alone in my bed because I couldn't shout for help through the ridiculous quantities of blood. After the operation, I dreamt of nothing at all because I was on an absolute shitload of painkillers.

I stayed at my dad's house for a fortnight while I healed, because my mum worked full-time and I had been led to believe that I could choke to death on my own blood at any time of the day or night. My dad did not work, because he had Parkinson's, and so could be in the house all day fluffing my pillows and doling out my liquid codeine in a responsible – if shaky – manner.

I divided my time between the lumpy spare bed and the lumpy couch, drinking meal-replacement milkshakes three times a day and trying to focus my drug-blurry eyes on the TV. The duvets and pillow were synthetic, cheap things from Ikea, and I woke up every night slimed in sweat, kicking the covers to the floor, instantly goosebumped. I spent a lot of the time listening to podcasts, which were a new thing at the time; I'd listen to the same episode over and over because I always drifted asleep after a few minutes. I kept wiping at the corners of my mouth but they always felt slippery. Later I realised this was because they were constantly bleeding: during the operation I'd had tubes in my mouth to suction up saliva, and they had rubbed the skin raw. Those cuts took a lot longer to heal than my tonsils, and – annoyingly – my painkillers ran out first.

Time stretched. I was only there for two weeks, but I quickly fell into the rhythms. My dad slept until 10 a.m., snoring like a giant, then made his slow stumble downstairs to smoke a cigarette while leaning heavily on the back door frame. During the day I dozed and my dad channel-flicked, punctuated by getting up for a cigarette at the back door every half hour. Sometimes he switched off the TV and we both dozed while Radio 4 burbled in the background, beeping the hours. When the sun went down he made his way through two bottles of white wine and whatever film was showing without adverts, while I – again – dozed. At midnight we sloped up to our respective bedrooms and I fell into a dreamless sleep before my dad's snoring could begin.

He took good care of me. He ignored every piece of advice a doctor ever gave him, but he followed my treatment instructions to the letter. I was given all my medicine at the proper times. I had clean sheets and clean pyjamas. I was never hungry. I did not cough blood. I healed, and I left. I don't remember if I said thank you.

3

MY DAD WAS ill for years: Parkinson's disease, alcoholism, skin flare-ups, colds. None of it seemed serious. He joked that he'd outlive us all. And then the phone call one rainy Wednesday morning, post-coffee but pre-cornflakes, my feet cold on the kitchen tiles. I'd just left a message on my dad's answering machine, so I thought it was him. I answered with a smile, voice singsonging. Heard my uncle's voice say intensive care.

I was flustered, panicked, tears fattening at the base of my throat. I got lost on the way to the hospital, even though I have lived in this city for fourteen years. My girlfriend had to collect me in a taxi.

I spent the next three days reading my dad the *Just So Stories* because he read them to me when I was a child; the stories had mixed with the ones of his Nigerian childhood until I believed that the elephant's child (oh best beloved) was his friend.

The nurses said he was too hot, so they wrapped his hands in ice packs. Then he was too cold, so they strapped his feet into fur-lined booties. Every time he twitched his hand or rolled his eyes, I'd let out a sob of joy because this was it, he was waking up, we were going to have that dramatic moment. He'd see how strong I was being. He'd see that I was looking after him the way he'd always looked after me. But none of it mattered – not the stories, not the drama – because he never woke.

On Saturday night, the doctor herded us into a little room – my dad's ex-wife, two children, girlfriend, and brother – and told us he had tonsillar cancer. Very rare. Very advanced. Treatment involves removing portions of the jaw and soft palate. If he made it out of intensive care, he'd be right back in with the treatment, which coupled with his other health problems would kill him. We agreed to turn off the machines.

It took minutes. I wanted to collapse onto him, to scream and sob and rage at the sky. But life is not like that. No one wants to make a scene.

Instead we huddled around his hospital bed, unsure of what to say. He still had towels around his hands and I was scared to remove them in case the nurses had done something to them. I imagined dried blood, open sores, sinister valves. I put my hand on his arm. I wanted him to see that I was brave. His skin was yellow and felt clammy like raw mushrooms.

And then he was gone, and I stared at his chest, at the way it did not rise, and I kept staring like I stare at the fake corpses on *CSI*, because you can always catch out the actors if you just keep staring. I stared, and I stared, and his chest did not rise.

I waited for the story to be over. I'd spent my life with my head in a book, seeing the world filtered through narrative, living fictional lives more often than my own. One thing I had learned about stories is that they always ended.

And at first, there was a strange pleasure in playing the character of Girl with Dead Father. No one expected anything of her but sadness. She did not have to go to work or worry about the gas bill or be nice to people. There's an odd beauty to grief: the pale cheeks, the gleaming eyes, the weight of sadness. Everything I said seemed more profound, more intense. Every childhood memory was tragic.

My mother, brother and I spent our days poring over old photos – still lifes of my father as a university student, as a twenty-something with my long-haired mother, holding a hundred versions of me as I stretch from a baby gurning on his lap to a teenager with my arm slung reluctantly around his shoulders.

All I wanted was a white bed. Cool sheets. A flannel on my forehead. I wanted nothingness. I wanted days measured by the sunlight moving from one side of the floor to the other. I didn't think then of Woodilee, but I thought of something like it. A ward of iron-frame beds with crisp bedding, my body tucked in, warm, and my face cooled by a breeze from the open window. Nurses' shoes squeaking on polished floors. The rattle of pills. A glass medicine cabinet, a ring of iron keys. Perhaps taking the air in a manicured garden; someone to push my chair and show me the different types of flowers. No one would expect anything of me. No one would even know I was there. I could stop time, and rest, and not think. Everything would be white and clean and nothing.

But also, that white bed, those cool sheets, that flannel on my forehead: not nothingness, but childhood. Being taken care of. Giving up all pretence at being a Proper Adult and doing Proper Adult things and just letting go, going back. I know that someone always had to be the grown-up, but I didn't want it to be me.

Two weeks passed and I tried to shrug off the costume of Girl with Dead Father, tried to shut the book and move on to another. But it was not a story, and it would not end.

I tried to write my dad: a fictional him, a man he would not recognise because he never saw himself there in the hospital. He never knew I read him 'The Elephant's Child'. He never knew his hands felt clammy like mushrooms. I wrote my father, and he became a story, and that is all I can have of him.

4

MY DAD ALWAYS wanted to be a writer. He wrote, but he wasn't a writer. He never published a book – or finished one, as far as I know. After he died I got all his papers. There were boxes full of photographs, documents, notes, journals. It was easy to make a story out of them. He may not have written stories, but he lived them.

In the month after he died I tried to go through it all. I'd put a Nick Drake CD on the stereo we'd inherited from him – a fancy one, Bang & Olufsen, the sort of thing I'd never buy even if I could afford it; it's so heavy I can barely lift it, and the CD player part has smoked glass doors that slide open when you wave your hand in front of them. I've seen it in the background in several films as part of fancy people's home decor. It's still the most expensive thing I own. I'd put on a Nick Drake CD, which was the

79

only music the whole family could ever agree that we liked, and so we played it at his funeral, and now I can't listen to it any more without crying. Back in the days of iPods, I got mine engraved with 'pink pink pink pink pink moon', and I still own it even though it doesn't work, just for that engraving. I'd put on 'Northern Sky' and 'Time Has Told Me', and I'd sit at the coffee table with a cup of coffee, all businesslike as if I was sorting out bills, and I'd start reading his journals. Within ten minutes I'd be sobbing, and I'd tell my girlfriend it didn't make sense, I shouldn't still be upset, it had been months now. And she'd hear the music and see the spreadeagled notebooks on the coffee table and tell me that of course I was upset, reading my dead dad's journals and listening to funeral music, you absolute crazy girl, who wouldn't cry at that? So I put the journals away, and I cried.

I wouldn't be a writer now if it wasn't for my dad. The same is true of dozens of other influences in my life; but I can trace my love of books and words straight to him. When I was little, instead of singing me lullabies he'd read me poems. My favourite, because it was his favourite, was T.S. Eliot's 'The Love Song of J. Alfred Prufrock'. Now that I think about it, perhaps it wasn't his favourite; it was just one that he'd been forced to memorise at school, so when his insomniac child whined for a story, it came easily to mind. I can still recite the opening stanzas, and in my head I hear it in his voice. I didn't understand the poem then, and at thirty-three I think I'm still too young to really understand it, though when he was reciting it to me he was only thirty-six and I thought he had all the wisdom the world could ever provide.

My favourite line of my favourite poem featured women talking of Michelangelo. I had never heard of the painter Michelangelo; the only Michelangelo I knew was the Teenage Mutant Ninja Turtle, so I assumed that's who they were talking of.

When I read the poem now, there are so many lines that resonate differently, and the one I keep coming back to, because it's how I feel every time I try to write about my dad or about Woodilee, conveys the impossibility of communication: that what is understood is not meant.

Later – years rather than months, in a new flat and with a new girlfriend who later became my wife – I did read my dad's journals. A story in my third book, 'Soon It Will be Cold Enough to Start Fires', was inspired by his words, and I used several phrases and images from a journal he kept on a family holiday when I was five. He never became a writer, but now he's a posthumous co-author. I know it's not much. But I'm trying.

I wish my dad had grown old. I wish he had worn the bottoms of his trousers rolled. I wish he had eaten peaches and heard the mermaids singing, each to each. I think they would have sung to him.

5

THE TRUTH IS that I never went back to Woodilee. I can't; it's not there any more. Now it's Woodilee Village, an estate of boxy red-brick new-builds with satellite dishes and laundry spinners and plastic Wendy houses in the garden. The clock tower is gone. The infinity track is gone. The ghosts are gone.

As soon as developers started tearing down the old buildings and putting up the bones of new ones, my interest in Woodilee disappeared. I thought about it – dreamed about it – but I never wanted to see it again. Even a glimpse of it would spoil the image of it that lived so vividly in my memory. Now when I get the Glasgow to Edinburgh train, I sit on the right-hand side of the carriage, so I don't even catch a glimpse of what it is now. It's only in writing this that I realise I do that.

*

I don't want to think that anyone lives there now.

I don't want to think that anyone else ever went there.

Woodilee exists only for me and my dad, turning infinity symbols in a little red Cinquecento.

A Glasgow Sang

Paul McQuade

PAUL McQUADE is a writer and translator from Glasgow, Scotland. His work has most recently been published in *Structo*, *Little Fiction*, the anthology *Out There*, and has been shortlisted for The White Review and Bridport prizes. He is the recipient of the Sceptre Prize for New Writing and the Austrian Cultural Forum Prize.

For Isa, and Nan, and Nana Fay,
for Margaret, and Agnes,
for Gina, and Gerry,
for Alison, and Mick.
I am proud to be your son.

EIGHT WOMEN ON Kelvin Way Bridge, frozen in time. The wind sighs in the folds of their robes, the drape of their sleeves. Their hands hold totems to the grey air of a Glasgow May: a spinning wheel, a child, a tiller, a hull, a mallet, a skull, a lute, some coins, a sledgehammer. They are not statues of women, but of ideas, gathered around four lamplights in pairs: Peace and War; Navigation and Shipbuilding; Philosophy and Inspiration; Commerce and Industry.

The lamps are not lit for the spring afternoons, but at night electric bulbs cast long shadows along the latticework of the iron bridge. Globes of moonlight, clearer than the ruddy amber that floods the rest of Glasgow's streets. There was a time when this bridge was lit by gas. It seems implausible that barely a generation ago men walked up and down the streets of this city, lighting the lamps with wicks on poles.

We take it for granted now, our electric simultaneity. The lamplighter is a forgotten profession.

My granda used to work as a lamplighter, after he worked the buses but before he was a miner. I wonder if he ever walked this bridge, in the shadow of Glasgow University, its grand spire and the bridge's ornate ironwork a world away from our lives in the East End. Had he crawled across the hull in Shipbuilding's hands, stared at the skull in which Philosophy gazes, reminding herself of the transience of life while he lit the lamp by her head and cast the sockets into deeper relief?

It would have been painful if he did. Not that granda ever knew anything about philosophy – the pain wouldn't have been for the *memento mori* in Philosophy's hands, but the arthritis in his right. He had to get injections in his wrist for it. Afterwards, his arm would be in a plaster cast, what we call, in Glasgow, a *stookie*.

It was while his arm was in a *stookie* that my granda fought the head of one of Glasgow's gangland families. Some trouble between the man's son and my brother. The man's wife showed up at my gran's door, screaming, her husband standing off to the side so that when my gran opened the door he could pull her out into the street and demand she produce my brother. It was at this point that my granda appeared – a bull charging from the doorway, a wolf snarling in the den – and knocked him on his arse. *Stoated him a belter*, my gran will tell me later.

A family legend. And true, at that. Only, at the time, my mum had to stay up all night, *feart*, sure that at any moment they were going to come back and shoot us, lock our doors and burn the house down with us inside. For weeks after, that man came by the house, walking his dog outside and looking in the windows with a blackened eye.

My granda died when I was too young to remember him. He lives in my life as this legend, among others.

The time a boy broke into the house to escape from a gang. The gang came in after him, smashing their way through, not realising he had already escaped through the back. My granda stood on the stairs, throwing punches while they tried to get past him, up to where his three daughters lay crippled with fear.

The time he was thrown from a mineshaft by an explosion at the pit in Cardowan. The accident was the third major one at the pit, and injured forty-seven.

His face appeared on the news so burnt and swollen not even his daughters recognised him. His airways had been scorched from inhalation, in a shaft so small it was impossible to run from the flames that threw him clear and left the skin on his back a melted ruin.

Of my own memories, there are only two: him turning to go up the stairs of a different house, and his bald spot, which made me think of Friar Tuck's tonsure in *Robin Hood*. And the second, when I visited him in the hospital as he lay dying of lung cancer after years down the pit. He was a man who survived gangsters, Thatcher, and explosions. He was forty-seven when he passed, on the seventh of June, the seventh son of a seventh son. Gerald Duffy. I was not there to see him turn and go, see his bald spot as he left, for the final time.

*

There is a charm to Upstate New York, where I stay at present, finishing my PhD. And in Tokyo, where I taught English while doing my Master's, there is an energy, a vastness, an air of possibility. But even in these cities, there are times when, far from Glasgow, I ache to hear its speech, to see the people, to feel the charge in the air that I have never found elsewhere. Other times, I barely notice that I am far from the city I was born in. There is work to do, people to see. And then I come home for a while – a few months, here and there, when I can – and I walk these streets, to see the changes that have happened while I've been gone, to see what's new, how it's grown. And as I take my coffee and go back out on the street, ready to wander, it feels as if all the memories I have of this place walk with me, like ghosts.

I walk up Ingram Street towards the Gallery of Modern Art, its pillars narrowed by the perspective of the street's long approach. The square in which it sits was once the centre of the tobacco markets, which, along with the shipyards, drew Glasgow from destitution to the second city of the Empire. Now, Royal Exchange Square is strewn with fairy lights, and coming into the open from between the tall buildings, a sudden sense of sky.

I sit on the edge of the steps in front of the gallery, to watch the traffic go past the statue of Duke Wellington. *The Equestrian State of the Duke of Wellington* is its full title, something I like to remind myself of whenever I see the Duke, sitting on his steed, proud and imperious, his brow topped with an orange traffic cone. This is the diadem Glasgow gave him in the early 1980s. It represents, they say, the Glaswegian spirit of humour and defiance in the face of authority. It was this same spirit that Thatcher would try, and fail, to break.

Such strange turns history takes. Wellington, born in Dublin, would become one of Britain's greatest military commanders, celebrated the length and breadth of the isles. And now he sits in this square, his majesty humbled by a municipal dunce cap. Thatcher herself – the Iron Lady – will inspire a young Nicola Sturgeon to take up the fight for Scottish Independence. Nicola Sturgeon, who now sits First Minister of a devolved Scottish Parliament, reconvened in Edinburgh after an almost three-hundred-year hiatus as part of a devolution process pursued by Labour to calm the storm Thatcher brought to Scottish civil waters.

'*Haw hen, gonnae hawd up,*' a man shouts, shuffling after a woman who rolls her eyes in impatience. They are heading towards the bus stop on Ingram Street, back the way I just came. She throws her arms down, and her eyes to the sky, clearly desperate to get out of the rain. But his steps are too short to keep up. People move at a different pace to history. They don't live in eras, but in these faltering steps. The dreich drudge of the day by day.

The woman runs ahead to catch the bus before it leaves the stop, asking the driver to wait. In a surprising gesture for a Glasgow bus, the driver obliges. I stand up to go as the doors shut behind him, with no direction, but an itch in my feet. They, at least, seem to know where they want to go – along Queen Street, to George Square.

There are few major statues in Glasgow, but those we have are gathered in this square, which sits before the City Chambers. George Square is busiest at Christmas, when the market comes, but now, it is empty, open, a few people on benches eating sandwiches, the pigeons stirring on the statues. Who do we celebrate here? Not ideas but men: Thomas Graham, Thomas Campbell, Lord Clyde, Sir John Moore, James Watt, Robert Peel, William Gladstone, Robert Burns, and James Oswald. Masters of art, industry, and empire. There are statues also of Victoria and Albert, but these are an irrelevance next to the towering spire on which Sir Walter Scott stands.

Looking up at Sir Walter Scott, I feel, not proud, but a slight sense of humour – mixed, perhaps, with a little defiance – that it is a writer who takes pride of place in this square, that there are poets here on the same podia as kings and queens.

How is it I have never read a word of Scott? Not *Ivanhoe*, not even *Waverley*. I was educated in a Scottish education system, and yet I never read a word of Scottish Literature – saving, of course, Burns, every January over haggis. The Ploughman's Poet as pittance. It was only in my final year of secondary school, in Advanced Higher English, that we were introduced to the work of Muriel Spark and Edwin Morgan. A belated discovery. Morgan, especially, is important to me. His spirit, his invention.

Other people, I suppose, encounter literature in the home, but no one in my family is a reader. My early education was conducted under the auspices of Section 28, which prohibited the advocacy of homosexuality – meaning any acknowledgement of its existence – from 1988 to 2000 in Scotland. Is this what exiled Morgan from our classrooms? But then, Morgan is only one of many.

Proper education meant looking upward, it seemed: to England, America, and canon. I remember Hughes, Orwell, and Shakespeare, but no MacDiarmid, Grassic Gibbon, or Gray. I do remember, however, Danny Boyle's adaptation of *Trainspotting* burning through our lives like wildfire. Renton's monologue from 'Relapsing: The Glass' memorised and recited, speaking something true about culture and politics to people who had until then had no interest in – or felt they had no part in – politics or culture.

Ten years after I left school, I found myself at La Sorbonne for the summer. During the day, we listened to philosophers in ancient, unventilated rooms, and at night, went for drinks in the still sweltering air of the city. In a bar near the Luxembourg Gardens, a woman from Canada told me how much Liz Lochhead's 'Bairnsang' meant to her. A *bairnsang* is a children's poem – *bairn* meaning *child*, *sang* meaning *poem* – about a child's first days of school, where she names the world in demotic; the poem then switches, the demotic being erased by education, meaning Standard English. Reading Lochhead's poem, I found there, as though waiting, some small piece of myself.

I could have read Scott in the thirteen years since school. In Edinburgh, where I lived for four years, there is also a monument dedicated to this man, the world's largest monument to a writer. And still, looking at him, here, in George Square, I have no interest. He seems too distant, too Romantic. It isn't for Scott that I've come.

What am I looking for, here, among these men of George Square?

A girl in a yellow cagoule is skipping through puddles across the brick-red paving. Her grandparents watch from the bench behind as she plays in Scott's shadow. The dour bronze, the grim facades of Edwardian sandstone, gargoyles and roses and the forbidding face of the City Chambers. And there she is, bright and lemon and wheeling through this place like it belongs to her.

Men. Save for Victoria, they are all men, these statues. But then, the proper names of history always seem to be. So few statues of women, unless she is a representation: Philosophy, Industry, Commerce, Liberty. Even the institution of the Crown.

Where are the women who have shaped the century?

The final lines of Lochhead's *sang* speak from my bones in response. When we speak a language, Lochhead says, it's one thing. But writing it – the way it *has* to be said – means to speak as though you were posh, grown-up, male, English, and dead.

*

Fibreglass, not bronze. Painted fibreglass: a woman on a pedestal, arms raised in defiance, and her dress, oddly angular, vaguely reminiscent of a nun's habit. Arthur Dooley, the artist who created it, had wanted bronze, but couldn't afford it. He couldn't even afford the fare to Glasgow to see it unveiled. It was a politicised project, opened in secret, with the Conservatives vowing to destroy it if they ever unseated the city's Labour council. This feat they have never accomplished. The statue survives, and was even renovated in 2010, with a small ceremony here at the Custom House Quay by the River Clyde. A monument to commemorate the Red Clydeside. A monument to a woman in Glasgow, and one who had never set foot here: Dolores Ibárruri, better known to history as La Pasionaria.

I first heard her name in Madrid. A friend was explaining to me the significance of the colour purple, *morado*, a word which surprised me in its distance from 'violet', the source of the colour in French and Italian. The Spanish is from *mora*, or mulberry, which made me imagine dark fruits, lined up in a row, bursting with juice. The way the purple bar of the flag of the Second Republic hung in the gallery with its forbidden colour, I imagined that if I touched it, my hands would come away stained.

Beside *la bandera*, under glass, was a banner from the siege of Madrid. The sign proclaimed: *¡No Pasarán!*

They shall not pass.

It was then that my friend told me the story of Isidora Dolores Ibárruri Gómez. The working-class seamstress who rose to lead the resistance in Spain against Franco. Who, after Franco took Madrid – *hemos pasado*, he said, *we have passed* – fled to the Soviet Union to live in exile, but returned after Franco's death to become a member of parliament at the age of eighty-two.

There is one incident from La Pasionaria's political career which has always stuck with me. In Asturias, long before the Battle of Madrid, La Pasionaria walked among the shells of buildings, the bullet-holes along the walls and the bodies hidden in soft, secret soils after an uprising stopped by Franco with such violence that it earned him the nickname *el verdugo*, the executioner. Franco the butcher of Asturias. From the wreckage, La Pasionaria gathered a hundred children to be taken from Asturias to Madrid. Political orphans. Their parents had been killed or jailed for revolutionary treason in Oviedo. Unable to make it to Madrid without herself being arrested, she eventually managed to send the children to the Soviet Union. There are bloodlines across Central and Eastern Europe, and further still, that owe their planting to the seeds La Pasionaria scattered.

I imagine this task must have been especially important to her – a personal significance. La Pasionaria buried four of her five girls at a young age, in coffins fashioned from fruit crates, and would later lose her son at the Battle of Stalingrad. Rescuing those children must have meant a lot to her. A retaking of power from the helplessness of Franco's rule, failed strikes, and the shadow of four small bodies laid to rest in boxes that might once have stored lemons.

Shortly before his death, Federico García Lorca was having coffee with La Pasionaria and some friends in Madrid, taking her in quietly, the way poets do – some secret conversation between perception and the word – and said: 'Dolores, you are a woman of grief, of sorrows... I'm going to write you a poem.'

I don't know if Lorca ever did write a poem for Dolores. But there is a comet named after her.

I imagine Lorca, on that Madrid street, looking at the tilt of her head, seeing a determination that steeled the jaw while she spoke. And sadness. He saw so much sadness in her. I can understand his inspiration. When I first encountered La Pasionaria that day in Madrid, I vowed I would write something about her myself. Not hagiography, but simply the image of a woman refusing to bend, a pair of seamstress' scissors, and a fruit box once used to hold lemons. History as the cutting and tying of thread, like the gossamer passed between the Fates. Only this time in mortal hands, weaving a pattern of grief held together with strength. These were the things that sang to me.

Imagine my surprise to learn, after years of neglecting the idea, that in my city, La Pasionaria is one of only three statues dedicated to a woman – Victoria, La Pasionaria, and the philanthropist and advocate of women's education, Isabella Elder, local hero of Govan. Here, far from home, Dolores stands, on the Clydeside in exile, her arms raised to the water.

Below La Pasionaria's feet lies a dedication, telling me that Glasgow and the British Labour Movement honour the men and women who fought fascism in Spain. At the time of the statue's construction, the Conservatives in Glasgow treated it with disdain, in keeping with the policy pursued by Stanley Baldwin, who advocated non-intervention in the Spanish Civil

War. The Conservatives feared that the Popular Front would spread Communism to Great Britain. There was resistance, of course. But not enough.

And now here she stands, alone by the water, named the way a saint is named: La Pasionaria. Her words sound silent now, across the Clyde. The skyline is changed since the shipyards began to moulder; the city alive again since the eighties and since Devolution. There is change in the air.

And yet, my relation to the Clyde is an uneasy one. It is the heart of Glasgow, with the firth for its aorta, where paddle steamers once carried people back and forth from the city to Brodick. Few ships now cross this water, to which the fortunes of Glasgow were for so long tied, when trade was bound to navigation, and the spoils of empire came and went with the tide.

One morning, my great-great-grandmother got her three daughters ready for school – fixed their hair with ribbons and pins, polished the worn leather of their shoes – and once she had said goodbye and left a kiss on each cheek, she walked down to the river and threw herself in. A neighbour jumped in after, trying to save her. A boy, nineteen. Both died.

Later, her daughter Isa repeated this gesture. She threw herself in a loch. It was my granda who had to go identify the body. Both fire and water render a body unrecognisable. A stranger to itself. The scars on his back and the swelling of her face. To this day, my mum tells me that drowning is an ugly death.

And then there is the other kind of drowning, the slow dissolution that has long plagued this country. Every country with poverty has its share of drunks. Religion is the opiate of the masses; but god or no god, opium is opium. Heroin, glue, or whisky; there are many ways to soften the hard edges of the world. These suicides are slower, but the death is still the same.

My great-aunt Agnes drank herself to death. She used to work as a chef at The Ashfield Club in Springburn, before the drink stopped her. They found her body on my ninth birthday, in her flat in Springburn, where I used to stay over and watch a VHS of *Captain Planet* rented from the video store. I remember, when the things were cleared from the flat, my mum talking about how they had to leave the mattress out, by the bins, for the cleansing, and how it was stained with all the mess that comes with death. She was a woman, a mother – she was loved. The alcohol took that at the same time it took her pain, leaving, in the end, nothing but that mattress. It is hard to think of it being left like that. In the shilpit judgment of the open air.

These are not the suicides of water I think of, when I think of, for example, Woolf, stones in her stout coat pockets, sure-footed, chin held high as she went to meet death. This is more desperate. A throwing, an attempt of a life to free itself from itself. From poverty, from suffering, from the chains of the mind.

What might my great-great-grandmother have done if she had had the kind of strength La Pasionaria held? Would she still have thrown herself into the river, leaving three daughters to be raised in a children's home?

Of the three, two committed suicide. Isa in the loch, Nan out a window. My great-gran, Nana Fay, was the only one of the three to live, though by the time I knew her she was no longer in a children's home, but a council house also in Springburn where she lived with my great-aunt Margaret. By that time, for Nana Fay, dementia was already beginning to blur the line between the present and the past and the here and now.

I used to visit her, in the nursing home she was moved to with Margaret, when things got so bad they could no longer look after themselves. A nursing home, a children's home. Maybe it was a blessing she wasn't present to the situation, that she couldn't see how her life had come full circle, to a room of musty armchairs and aging bodies. People forgotten while they were still alive.

*

I move across the water from La Pasionaria, over the bridge towards Glasgow Green and The People's Palace, opened in 1898 to help develop the East End, at the time suffering from an epidemic of illness and overcrowding. The People's Palace Museum is different to the monuments of George Square, different even to the statue of La Pasionaria. The People's Palace does not attempt to remember an individual, but social life, how people live, how things changed and are changing. It chronicles the reorganisation of society, though whether this is, as the great Scottish Socialist of the early twentieth century, John Maclean – whose writing desk is stored there – once said, in the movement of the people gaining the world and retaining it, or, on the other hand, of the world being taken from them, depends on the decade and your point of view.

Given the span of history, and the shape of Scottish politics, I wonder what Maclean would have thought, had he lived to see the Labour movement rise in Scotland, with Glasgow the city it long considered its stronghold. He would have seen the great Labour projects of home rule and worker's rights bear fruit. And then, later, after the seventies and Thatcher and North Sea oil, he would also have lived to see Labour begin its decline in Scotland, losing a forty-year control of Glasgow City Council for the first time in 2017. The SNP are a new force in Scottish politics. Their first MP was elected in 1945, though it wasn't until Winnie Ewing won the Hamilton by-election in 1967 that the party had any real success. Now it is dominant in Scottish politics, overseeing a devolved parliament. The political project launched at the turn of the century has seen generations die before it could be achieved, so many dreams passed over to people who will never know what they have inherited. So many lives lost in churning water.

The Clyde has seen all this, though I can't imagine that it thinks much of it. The Clyde is ancient – it was the heart-blood of the Kingdom of Strathclyde, or Alt Clut, long before its water ever touched a place called Glasgow or any people who called themselves

Scots. It has seen emperors, kings, queens; it has seen
the rise and fall of dynasties, peoples, Gaels, Picts,
Romans; it has seen two world wars and blood and
ash and the long nights of bombs. It has had its veins
opened for the ships that will develop, then ruin, the
city. And still, it is as it is: forever flowing into the
dark.

What will it face in a century? What history will
be written here?

It is hard to think that, given all that has passed
in the city, I still feel a personal connection to this
water. One death is meaningless on such a large scale.
But then, humans do not live in historical time. We
are alive in our own personal way, and the personal
is always more painful. Maybe this is what I like
most about The People's Palace. It tells us that it is
important to remember people, to think about how
connected we are. How indebted we are to the past
and the dead we never meet.

I wonder what these dead ancestors would think if
they met me. If they would be proud of the person I
am, and am trying to become. We tend to think of history as continuation, but generation upon generation
we become strangers to each other. In Glasgow, this is
more pronounced. The Glasgow Effect, the term used

for persistent early mortality without socioeconomic correspondence, cuts many lines short in their prime. In 2016, an artist born in west London, but settled in Glasgow, will name an art project after this, the premise being that she wouldn't leave Glasgow for a year in order to demonstrate the interconnectedness of the art world. She did not understand the outrage she caused, naming a project this while receiving funding to live in a city where others have no choice but to stay, and others struggle to make rent. A performance of privilege as punishment. A profound and insensitive obliviousness. The Glasgow Effect has consequences; it changes Glasgow's sense of time. A generation here is different to a generation elsewhere. Things move quicker, break faster. We all die, of course. Just some of us sooner than others.

And what lives might they have lived, those who died too early? What might they have made of themselves? Where hope is denied it finds itself given over, across the years, as an inheritance. An ember burning in the mind.

My father had a brilliant mind. But a brilliant mind in Barrhead – *Bawrheid* – with five brothers and a sister has a tendency to go nowhere. It was only later, when we were kids, that he went to night school, so he could get a better job and we could have a better life. He got a low mark in only one module: economics. Because his tutor opposed Keynesianism, which, to my father, was the soundest form of economy.

My mother did well in languages, and art, though she always wanted me or my brother to become doctors. A dream she had for herself, before life got in the way. Practicalities. She and my dad met at entry-level jobs in a bank when they were still teenagers, where they worked the majority of their lives. Her own dreams seemed impossible to her, being where she was from, and then grew more unreachable when she had a young family. Her children came first.

My great-aunt Margaret was a brilliant typist. In the Second World War she received a medal from the Queen for her efforts, before she suffered a stroke from an alcoholism that robbed her of the use of her hands and left her epileptic, prone to fits where her mouth foamed and her body shook as if struck by lightning.

Einstein famously said that he stood on the shoulders of giants. Most of us stand on the shoulders of generations born huddled and broken, but living still, as best they could. But we love them no less. From them we inherit no less. A culture and a history. All that might have been.

My chest feels filled with seawater as I look out on the bridges that cross this river, thinking of how many people have crossed it with the promise of their life unfulfilled. We will never know them. Most of the memories that once held them are dead themselves. And if not, their histories lie in family archives, in stories told at Hogmanay or whenever a bottle loosens a tongue.

I suppose this is what The People's Palace attempts to preserve; if not the histories, at least their connections. *Fae the steamie tae the dancin*, there are many shadows, breakings, and tragedies. But the heart still beats its rigour, in the end. This is the city. This is the energy of people living together. All it needs is purpose.

This is what all the great socialists of history have tried to unlock. I think of Mary Barbour, and her army, charging through these streets to the Sheriff Court, in the Great Rent Strike of 1915. Women united in claiming justice and a better life from landlords bleeding them dry while their husbands died at Flanders. What would Mary Barbour have thought,

come the fall of the Berlin Wall, and all the secrets
that crawled from the rubble?

Of all the revelations that came when the Iron
Curtain was drawn back, there is one from Romania
that I have never been able to shake. Ceauşescu made
the people carve wooden fruit and vegetables so they
could televise football stadia filled with them – to
demonstrate the success of the regime, and to show
the world how bountiful the People's Republic was.
Row upon row of golden corn, spilling carrots orange
as sunsets, and the full flowers of courgettes. Children
on their fathers' shoulders waving red flags and singing 'The Internationale'. All of them starving, forced
to carve and paint glossy red apples they could never
eat. I imagine some of them, in desperation, still took
a bite, thinking of Snow White, dreaming of sleep,
only to find their mouths filled with biting *skelfs*.
Splinters of wood in the red chamber of throat. Many
fled the post-Communist sphere to settle in Glasgow.
They chose this place to rebuild. They chose this
place to call home.

Looking at the water, I am reminded of how many
times Glasgow itself has been broken. It was targeted
heavily by the Luftwaffe because of the shipyards,
whole sections of the city reduced to rubble in the

Clydebank Blitz of 1941. Then, in its decline, the ship-yards will once against break Glasgow's heart. In the past years there have been no shortage of tragedies, it seems: the crash of a helicopter into the Clutha Vaults in 2013, killing ten, the bin lorry crash in 2014, six dead and fifteen injured, mowed down in the middle of their Christmas shopping.

On the Clutha Vault Mural, there is an image of Mary Barbour. Though efforts to erect a statue to her memory have failed, she is remembered there as part of a history. Of breaking, of grief, and of coming together.

I think of that woman standing by the water's edge all those years ago, after sending her three daughters off to school and then, later, their deaths. I wish I could give her the strength of Dolores Ibárruri and Mary Barbour. I wish I could give her a future.

*

When La Pasionaria was fighting in Spain, Edwin Morgan was receiving piano lessons in Pollokshields from a student named Lex Allan. Allan tells Morgan that, if he had been a little bit older, he might have gone to Spain to fight, like the English poets. They talk of Federico García Lorca, the poet who had wanted to compose a poem about the sadness of La Pasionaria. Openly gay, and famously infatuated with Salvador Dali, Lorca was killed shortly after the start of the Civil War in 1936.

But his name passed between Lex Allan and Edwin Morgan. Not even whispered, like a secret, but openly, without shame. A clear voice in hale air. Poetry a link between generations.

There is a statue dedicated to Lorca, on la Avenida de la Constitución in Granada, and a museum, originally his family's summer home, located in a park which bears his name. These are monuments dedicated to a poet murdered by Nationalist firing squad, and whose body was never found. In lieu of something to bury, they wrote his name in the heart of the city.

Edwin Morgan's name can be found mostly in libraries, especially in the University of Glasgow, where his name graces the Edwin Morgan Centre for Creative Writing, an institutional setting for creative practice about which Morgan was deeply ambivalent.

But Morgan's legacy goes beyond a name. He was the first Laureate of Glasgow, then the first national poet, the Scots Makar. His name is also on a plaque in the Scottish Parliament, bearing the poem he wrote for the opening of the building in 1999 – 'Open the Doors'. Between the break of 1707, to the reconvention of 1999, Morgan's poem forms a link and a remembrance: 'Dear friends, dear lawgivers, dear parliamentarians, you are picking up a thread of pride and self-esteem that has been almost but not quite, oh no not quite, not ever broken or forgotten.'

Between generations, this poem forms a link. It speaks its message long after the death of Morgan himself, after a long battle with cancer, finally succumbing to pneumonia in 2010 – the year in which I first read him. My English teacher, Mrs Thorpe, who had been one of his students, spoke of him with such love and such esteem that she made him seem alive in a way no other writer had.

There was a public service at Glasgow University, before a private cremation with his friends and family. His body was, in the end, reduced to ash, then scattered on Cathkin Braes. But between generations, writing forms a link. At his funeral, the last song sung was Burns' 'A Man's a Man for a' That'.

My dog stops sniffing the grass up ahead to turn and look at me as if she senses something in my thoughts. I clap her on the head as I come up, and she runs off again. She is slightly confused by the route we are taking today. A pilgrimage, of sorts.

By strange coincidence, I am related to Morgan by way of a death. His father, Stanley Morgan, died in Robroyston Hospital in 1965. Closed in 1977, the land was later developed as a new urban suburb. My family moved there in 1988 and live there to this day. It's a strange thought: Morgan coming to visit his father, dying, on the same ground where, later, I will read the poem he wrote in response to this death. 'Message Clear' is my first experience of Morgan. A concrete poem, it follows the sentence 'I am the resurrection and the life' from its breakdown through various permutations, like a crypt or cipher. A code in crisis.

I am the resurrection and the life.

I try and remember what I can of the poem. The first line is a question. It asks: *Am I?* I remember that. The question. And the answer: *I am rent if I am.*

This line sticks in my head because of the verb *render*. I can render a text in a language, say, when I translate it into English, but *to render* also means to melt down, like metal, to its basest elements. I suppose this is one way of thinking about translation: a productive breakdown in language.

The rend of the poem, of course, means to tear.

I am rent – I am torn in my sorrow. If I exist at all:
Am I?

It always seemed to me that Morgan's poem does
this to itself, that it rends and renders itself. And it
does this at the limit of a life, where his father lay
dying, believing that beyond – as if just out of sight,
or in shadow, as if it could be seen with the right light
– lay resurrection.

I am the sun. I am the son.

How painful had those lines been to write?

The dog has stopped to stare at a magpie, one paw
raised as if ready to run, tip of her white tail straight
in the air. I say hello to the bird, out of habit. A super-
stition I learned from my mum. One for sorrow, two
for joy.

At each step, I ask myself: Is this where Stanley
Morgan died?

I know of only one remaining piece of the former
hospital, an iron fence that lines the woods behind
my aunt's house. This marked the perimeter, but
the building layout can't be deciphered in this new
network of cul-de-sacs and red brick. The hospital
had been a smallpox hospital before a general one.
I remember a skull being upturned while someone

was building a conservatory. How many deaths do we live on here?

The dog and I make our way out of the old estate, where the hospital once was. The Campsie Fells loom on the horizon. More and more houses have risen in their shadow since I was young, new estates sprung up to accommodate the needs of Glasgow's growing population. We have a school now, a supermarket, a gym, though only two buses. They say a train station is coming. What will become of Robroyston then? It is as old as I am, this suburb. But its history – like the history of Glasgow itself – runs far deeper, though there is only one monument to this past.

In 1305, William Wallace took his last drink from a well in Rab Raa's Toun – now Robroyston – before the Bishop of Glasgow betrayed him in Bishopbriggs to the English. There is a small monument, a Celtic cross, some fourteen feet tall, and far from the well which has now fallen into decay, but which I passed every day in life on the way to school.

Looking at the monument, I am taken aback by a message left there. A Latin inscription: *Dico tibi verum libertas optima rerum, nunquam servili sub nexu vivito fili.*

I tell you the truth, the best of all things is freedom; never live under the bonds of slavery, son.

Is it a chance connection, this message from a father to a son?

I still remember when I was about twelve years old, my father told me he was happy that I don't sound like him or my mother. Something they had worked hard to achieve; that proper English was the only way I spoke. It meant that I would have a better life, he said. He had travelled down to London, once, for a meeting at the bank he worked for. After the meeting had finished, one of his colleagues took the manager aside to ask if they could fire my dad because they couldn't understand him on account of his accent.

Each father imparts the wisdom they think will serve best, I suppose. Wallace was a noble, Morgan middle-class. The lessons taught there are different. Middle-class families teach their children to be like them. They are comfortable not only economically, but with themselves. This is not always the case with working-class families. When my nephew turns to his granda and says, 'Speak properly', a small part of me breaks.

What I like most about 'Message Clear' is that, rather than take the sentence 'I am the resurrection and the life' as its starting point and following its breakdown, its failure to send, the poem begins in grief. An elemental crisis: *Am I?*

From there it builds. It finds a way to piece back together not simply the sentence, but things that were unimaginable when the sentence was whole. It finds strength in being broken. It finds a way to render itself in being rent. Writing becomes not simply a link between generations, but its own form of resurrection.

*

Few people in Glasgow remember The Hielanman's Umbrella. Or rather, they do not know that this is its name. But the railroad bridge at Central Station, distinctive in its Venetian glass windows, is immediately recognisable to anyone in Glasgow or anyone who has had to pass through below the station's famous clock.

I like to watch the anxious people waiting in the station whenever I have to wait for a train. The ones who are carrying bouquets, who step up and down on one foot, searching the crowd for that face – the one face they search for in every crowd. I like to see them come together, their steps quickening to the reunion. The great sweep of arms. The kiss, the spin. Again,

again. It makes me happy to see how people connect, here, to see people so unabashed in their love.

I remember getting off a train from Manchester and approaching my then-boyfriend with the same excitement. Only it blended into hesitancy before we kissed. I think I appreciate the openness of people in their affection because I envy them the fact that they can do so without fear. Every queer person knows that affection must pass a check. This isn't a matter of repression, but of survival.

I get a coffee to keep me warm as I wander, thanking the man serving me by saying: *'At's smashin ta.'* This is my immediate reaction to service; the baristas in New York laugh at me for it, because it sounds so quaint. British, even. But the prevalence of the term 'smashing' owes its history to Gaelic. *'S math sinn*, meaning: *it's good*. No matter how many people forget, or how many secrets sleep in language, you cannot undo the fact of diaspora. How many foreign tongues do we speak daily without knowing it? *Democracy*, Greek. *Parliament*, French. *Shampoo, bungalow, pyjamas*. How many words has English raided from Bengal?

We say *gruesome* without realising it is Scots. Popularised by Scott, in fact. And it was a writer's project, later, that would reinvigorate the language. MacDiarmid's great ambition was to synthesise Scots into a modern, systemised form. And who could deny him, that? Who wouldn't want to preserve words like *watergaw* for rainbow? Who cannot appreciate the guttural beauty of *howk, mocket,* and *caw canny?*

There are those who decry MacDiarmid for his construction of a 'synthetic' language – Lallans. But what is a 'natural' language? There is a famous anecdote, of a gathering at the Vatican, where the priests tried to speak to each other in their *lingua franca.* Latin was the same language, written down, but when it came to speaking it, the words were incomprehensible. Local language had deformed the Church's Vulgate. We now know these Latins as French, Spanish, and Italian. In this transformation, languages without name were preserved, as an echo. And here, in Glasgow, the bridge of the station – for now, at least – preserves the word *Heilanman*, the Scots word for a Highlander.

Heilanmen means anyone not a Lowland Scot, a distinction which was as important, at the time, as the distinction Scottish/English now. And conversely, to the *Heilanmen*, the word *Sassenach* referred, without distinction, to the Lowland Scots and English. People who had predated upon the North, destroyers of a life, a people, and a place. What we recognise within the borders of Scotland, now, was not so at the time. Without the myth of a country, we were all foreign to each other.

Walking through the crowd, the voices blend together. The edges of language bleed into a common pulse. The sign of a city alive with itself. Walking down to the lower platforms, I take the side entrance to the station and emerge below into the dark awning of the highlander's umbrella.

Gathered in Glasgow, the highlanders were forced to find work where they could in the wave of industrialisation, after being expelled from the land in which they had lived for generations. Some were sold as slaves, others to the kelp industry. Some emigrated, others fled. But for those who remained – those who could remain – they would gather together, in their exile, under this bridge. They would stay safe from the rain there, huddle together for warmth in shared breath and shared language. Their voices seem to echo, now, this dreich Monday, though I am separated from them by a century.

Gabh mo leisgeul, gabh mo leisgeul. Mas e do thoil

e. Tha mi gad ionndrainn gu mòr. Chan eil mi 'tuigsinn. Tha mi duilich. Mo ghaol ort.

I do not have the words to respond; I can only walk in the shadow of the umbrella and listen to its ghosts.

There is a common misconception that, due to the immense amount of laments in Gaelic song, that there is something inherently tragic about the Gaels. One hears so much talk of death. A dying culture, a dying – if not already dead – language. But walking beneath The Heilanman's Umbrella, I think of a song Mary MacPherson sang about shinty – *camanachd* – in Glasgow. It is not a lament, but a celebration, of the New Year and the boys playing on the field. She sings: *''S iad gillean mo ghràidh / Tha 'n Glaschu nan sràid / Is fhada bho àit' an eòlais iad.'*

These are the young men, dear to my heart, far from home, on Glasgow's streets.

Mary MacPherson was born in 1821, on Skye, the isle the Gaelic poets refer to as *eilean a' cheo*, the isle of mists. Like the name of Glasgow itself, all Gaelic speakers have names that turn themselves inside out: Mary MacPherson, Màiri NicDhòmhnaill, or as she was later known, *Màiri Mhòr nan Òran*, Great Mary of the Songs. She is one of the most enduring Gaelic poets. Sorley MacLean, in particular, was fond of her.

Mary lived in Glasgow for a time. Born on Skye, the city would be part of her exile, but she first left the island to work in Inverness as a maid, before she was falsely accused of theft and imprisoned. Afterwards she left the North and came to Glasgow, like the other *heilanfolk*, where she trained as a nurse and taught herself English.

Torn from the isles, the highlands, the glens, the *Heilanmen* lived in exile in Glasgow, gathering under this bridge to stay safe from the rain. Màiri herself, far from Skye, sings the songs of a people in exile, and in her voice makes a place for them. And when she finally returned to the land of her birth, she gathered the songs of her people, and she gathered her people. She led them in their resistance to the Sassenachs preying upon the land. She gathered and sang songs of pain and resistance, most notable being 'Eilean A' Cheo', a song named for Skye itself. Its mists and high mountains, the swans, the seals. The topoi of a tradition.

Mary sings in Gaelic: 'Who has ears, or a heart that beats with life, who will not sing this song with me, of the hardship that has befallen us?' She sings: 'Remember your suffering and keep your banner high, for the wheel of change will not turn for you without strength and hard hands.'

When people in Japan asked what kind of country Scotland is, I would often tell them that there were lots of sheep. I think this is a common sight in modern rural Scotland: blackfaced sheep wandering the hills. But to the Highlanders, the sheep came from the south like a plague, driving away farmers, the cattle and their herders, in order to produce wool for the booming looms.

From this distance in history, sheep seem like a quintessential aspect of the Scottish landscape. But to the Gaels, the sheep meant death.

It is strange, then, that in Japanese, I often mistake the word for sheep – *hitsuji* (羊) – with the word *hitsugi* (棺), meaning, *coffin*. More times than I can count, I have told people: Scotland is a country filled with coffins.

Scotland, country of coffins. Glasgow, city of ghosts.

*

The River Kelvin runs below, singing whatever song it is that water sings. Cousin to the Clyde, I have no relation to it – it separates the West of Glasgow from the centre, and I am from the other side of this division. I am in Kelvingrove Park, standing on the bridge that crosses the water, looking out at the leaves of the trees, so dark in their green that the grey rocks and water seem a part of them. Above me, to the right, Glasgow University towers. Morgan taught there from 1947 and lived almost his entire life on this side of the river, in Anniesland. My aunt, on the other hand, came to the West End for the first time last year – this is how circumscribed Glasgow life can be, from East to West and North to South.

It is a peculiar feature of small countries that such little distance can produce vastly different cultures. Edinburgh is fifty minutes away by train but a world away for all that. Until the introduction of economy air travel, most people travelled within reach of train or car. Economics confined them, but part of this also meant that they had a more thorough understanding of their geography. It is common nowadays for people never to explore a country but see simply its centres and resorts. Why go to Pitlochry when you can fly to Berlin? Why go to the Isles, with their temperamental ferries, when there is Malaga, the Bahamas, Seoul, Beijing? Economy still constricts us, but it's not quite the same. Modern tourism brings us farther, but fails to bring us understanding.

When my mum was young, her holidays were in Anstruther, or my gran and granda would go up the west coast. When I was two, Gina and Gerry took me over on the ferry to Arran, but I can't remember it. Somewhere inside me that day must have left an impression – the feeling of sea spray and the wind from the waves. I wish I could remember it. The three of us together.

I left Glasgow properly when I was seventeen, for university, then Scotland itself when I was twenty. Tokyo, then Upstate New York. I have spent half my life living elsewhere, in other tongues. My first foreign language was French, my second Japanese. After this came German. As for a first language, or a mother tongue, between Glaswegian and English there will always be a tension, a politics, and a problem of appearance.

The only language I remember my mum teaching me is French, when I was three. The creaking white leather of the couch, the dog milling around the floor, tail beating at our legs. *Une, deux, trois, quatre* . . . I remember a kind of bubbling glee, that hysterical laughter children have in the pleasure of pure nonsense. What were these sounds? *Une* was not *one* and definitely not *wan*. Along my fingers the words ran, as my mum taught me to count in a language neither of us spoke.

I think what attracted me to foreign languages was that they were untouched by British class politics, a world shaped by cultural contours that were independent of where I came from. I didn't understand this at the time. All I knew was that things seemed easier, a burden lighter, when I was speaking French. And the more competent I became in foreign tongues, which is to say, the less foreign those tongues became, the freer I felt in myself. There is nothing remarkable in moving between tongues – over sixty per cent of the world's population is at least bilingual – but every time I do, I feel a certain sense of freedom.

And yet I still remember a group of English men in Tokyo turning away from me, literally, when they learned I was Scottish. World travel and cosmopolitanism do not include the parochialism of a small country. I remember being confused, and hurt. Ashamed, somehow, to be who I was, or who they thought me to be: Scottish, parochial, and never enough. It was as though, no matter how far I went, there was no escape. There would always be a limit to freedom because I was always, in the end, me. It is in these moments that, rather than stand and fight, I want – desperately and despite myself – to escape who I am.

I moved to New York after Tokyo – Upstate, though the city is only five hours of nausea from the bus' antiquated suspension away – and still, just last year, I was out with an English friend when we got talking to a girl at the bar who was visiting, and also, it turned out, from England. Upon learning I was from Glasgow, she responded with: 'Oh, so you're scum.' I think a lot of people would be surprised how often these comments happen. Each time, the strangest thing is that the people who say them seem to expect a response.

On the night of the 2014 referendum, at a time when Scotland was electric with change, I stopped in a petrol station in New York with another English friend to buy beer for the night. By some strange coincidence, the woman working there was also English, but married to an American military man and had lived in the US for years. To my friend, she said: 'What do you think of them trying to take Scotland away from us?'

Sometimes I worry that my life is shaped by shame.

Of who I am, where I'm from, how I speak, whom I love. A shame of what I am and what I am not. A mongrel with five tongues and no fixed address. Sometimes, I look back and realise that, deep down, I was always trying to be: posh, grown-up, male, English, and dead.

As I grow older, I am trying to undo this. I take no pride in a nation, a soil, a blood, or even a language. I am trying to learn something different – a sense of self, the strength to appear. The strength to step off a train and be swept up in a kiss, in a moment, in love without fear. In this, I am reminded of Morgan, when he says: 'there is in love / a great strength; by it, indeed, we live. / And love is love whatever flesh it inhabits.'

Turning back to walk eastward through the park, I am confronted by a statue at the other end of the bridge. Dedicated to the memory of those who lost their lives in the Boer War. Looking at the man on the statue, poised with his gun on a rock, I recognise nothing of myself in it. Sometimes, in the West End, I feel as much of a foreigner as I do in Paris. But the statue makes me remember another monument, in Dublin: James Larkin, the great trade unionist, born in Liverpool to Irish parents. The memorial to 'Big

Jim' bears an inscription in three languages, reflecting the distance the French had to travel to take root on Irish soil. A message sent long-distance, carried across generations. Broken down then resurrected. The statue attests, in a multilingual proclamation, to a history and a strength.

Les grands ne sont grands que parce que nous sommes à genoux: Levons-nous.
Ní uasal aon uasal ach sinne bheith íseal: Éirímis.
The great appear great because we are on our knees: Let us rise.

*

The statue in Kelvingrove has put something in my mind, led me on a short detour through Nelson Mandela Place on the way back to the bus. The monument to the Boer War and the dedication to Mandela: a contradiction. Humour, and a little defiance.

It was the Boer War that established the future Republic of South Africa and its ensuing apartheid. I am reminded that, at the time, many Irish Republicans, seeing in the Boers the mistreatment of themselves, went to Africa to fight against the British. Glasgow's monuments always seem to give me an uneasy sense of my own history.

It was this war that will, in the end, be met with resistance in the 1980s, the city of Glasgow, the first among many – Aberdeen, Dundee, Newcastle, and Sheffield – to declare Mandela free despite his incarceration in Robben Island. Strange routes history takes. That massacre can lead to this joining – in the spirit of Mandela – to justice beyond the limits of the law. A slow arc, Martin Luther King Jr. would say. The anti-apartheid movement in Glasgow took nearly twenty years before this action could take place, a seed planted in part by the exile Cecil Williams, a South African who ended up living in Anniesland, the same place as Morgan, and who came into contact in Glasgow with Phil and Cathy Filling, part of the city's Labour and Communist movements. It is this connection that will help forge the movement that brought Mandela to the city upon his release.

Scottish schooling was never politically neutral: we learned about apartheid, about lynching in the USA, about Jim Crow laws and rapes in the South. We read *To Kill a Mockingbird* and *The Underground Railroad* and a novel about Pinochet. I can't remember the name, only one scene: a football stadium filled with corpses in an unnamed Latin American country the teacher will explain is Chile, before unpacking the history of the disappeared for us. Domestic issues were the only ones missing. We never learned about the sugar trade, Jamaica, the Raj. We never learned about empire. British History meant the Second World War, and our part in saving Europe from the tyranny of the Third Reich.

Thatcher was close to Pinochet, and her government opposed the dismantlement of apartheid, especially pressure by sanctions on the South African regime. Thatcher's husband Denis had business interests in the country. This is part of it. The other is ideological: Thatcher believed that only the apartheid system could protect the free market from communism. The price was worth paying, she said, which is easy to say when you don't have to foot the bill. There was resistance, but not enough.

I still remember being quietly stunned reading an interview with Mandela, in which he said Glasgow would always have a close place in his heart. I didn't understand, then, the connection he had to this city.

Though not there, any more, the South African General Consulate was located in St. George's Place, which was renamed Nelson Mandela Place in 1986 by the efforts put in place by Cecil Williams. Humour, and a little defiance.

There is, around the church in the square, a variety of shops, but the most important place is the blood donation centre. My mum used to receive constant calls and letters to donate because her blood is O negative. My blood is positive, which meant during pregnancy her immune system saw me as a foreign body.

When the South African General Consulate was here, Nelson Mandela Place was a political statement against apartheid. But I do not think that the blood centre is any less political. Blood flows here. Blood binds here. And not simply between generations – sometimes even a mother and child are separated by blood. But here in Nelson Mandela Place, the needle taps the vein, and blood begins its long flow from heart to heart, heedless of caste, creed, or colour.

I have never been to the blood centre in Nelson Mandela Place. Not out of fear of needles or any complacence; I am legally prohibited from donating. Too high risk. In the UK between 1999 and 2011, for over a decade, the rate of HIV transmission was higher through heterosexual intercourse, but the eighties cast a long shadow over our present. I understand this, but it is still disheartening to look at the blood centre; a grim prospect to think that the only way I could save someone would be if I died and my organs could be donated. I take some heart in knowing that if Morgan came here to give blood, then we would be side by side on the street outside, together in our exile.

Looking at the sign for Mandela Place, I am reminded, not of Glasgow's part in a global anti-apartheid movement, but of complicity; not just of a prime minister who would allow the regime to continue in the interests of the economy, but of Glasgow's complicity in slavery, of the tobacco lords who made this town, selling goods in Africa in exchange for slaves they would then sell in the Americas. Burns, the Ploughman's Poet, very nearly worked as a plantation manager in Jamaica out of economic considerations, where he would have overseen the work of slaves. And yet, this is the same poet who wrote 'The Slave's Lament', inspired by the Abolitionists' cause.

Some years ago, a Polish man introduced me to a performance of this song at Celtic Connections, a festival of traditional arts and culture held annually in Glasgow. Karine Polwart sang Burns with Alkinoos Ioannidis, a folk singer from Cyprus, performing a lullaby in Cypriot Greek. Ioannidis begins the performance: a bare voice, impossibly fragile. Then Polwart joins, and the two songs join, the voices thread and strengthen each other. Burns' song, a lament from a slave bound to Virginia, is marked by the line 'And alas! I am weary, weary O', while the lullaby responds with an invocation of St Marina to let a child sleep. Across time and language, at an unexpected juncture, the song forms a link between generations. Its notes sounding across distance and diaspora. And in this connection, it attempts to find some form of comfort.

*

My parents weren't readers but they always encouraged it. A way for us to better ourselves. Put it down to the old Socialist-Catholic tradition of Glasgow's East End, or chalk it up to working-class ambition – the page was where, like Larkin said, we could rise. My relationship to literature, and to language, will always be coloured by this. By the promise of being better than we were, more than we are.

For many years, I was obsessed with English grammar. I would read every explanation the early Microsoft Word gave me for green underlines, absorb every rule they taught us in school. To this day my skin crawls at the death of the subjunctive mood, or the common confusion between lay and lie. This is something left over, a prescriptiveness I can't shake, connected to the feeling of being *wrong*. This is a linguistic as much as a sexual predicament, wrapped up in the boundaries of class. Wrongness along three lines. Unbelonging.

I wanted to be correct; to feel correct for once. I thought knowing all the answers of this riddle we call English would finally allow this. How different might my life have been if I had read Morgan's translation of Jean Racine's *Phaedra* into Glaswegian, or Mayakovsky into Scots? Tom Leonard's 'Six O'Clock News'? Lochhead's 'Bairnsang'? How many people's lives would be changed by finding dignity in themselves, instead of only confusion, pain, degradation, and shame?

But these were not the books I read. My father taught me to read early, and we read *The Hobbit* and *The Lord of the Rings* together when I was three; these were the books I practised on, the world I loved to be in, so far away from our real lives. But I remember reading these books myself, for the first time, these familiar books, and the feeling I had of the words on the page: they sounded so different, in my head, to the voices around me, that for a minute it felt as though someone else were speaking in my brain.

Later, this will be a familiar experience: whenever I am in another language, my brain picks up sentences, new vocabulary, turns of phrase, and repeats them inside my skull. The words sink down and become part of me. They change how I sound, the way I speak. Voice and accent are malleable. Even the timbre of the vocal cords, over time, deepens with wear. Nothing in language is static; it moves like the tide, changing the landscape in slow, soft movements. I think you become more receptive to this, when you are born between idioms.

People say that you never know Glasgow until you speak with a 'Glasgow accent' and I suppose this is true, to some extent. There is a Glasgow that exists only in Glaswegian. A way of speaking and a battery of expressions that bind us in a common memory. But like any language, it is a door. It appears as a wall, at first, but can always be opened, if you're willing to learn – the difference between *naw* and *nae* and *yin* and *wan*, what it means to say *wheesht, glecks, oaxters, lum, caw canny, stooshie, here you hum, haw urr ye, n'ahm urrnae, a sair heid, gie's wan, och, loupin, a coupin, ye dancin? aye ah uhm.*

There is that Glasgow, but there are many others. There is a Glasgow of Glaswegian. A Glasgow of Scottish English and of Scots, of Gaelic, of British Standard and all its permutations. A Glasgow of French, Spanish, Italian. A Glasgow of Farsi, of Urdu, of Mandarin, of Cantonese, Japanese, and Korean, of Xosa, of Turkish, of Polish, of Hungarian. And underneath these trappings, language without nation, a million dialects cutting the rough diamond of voice. Sparks catching kindling in the dark.

*

It is hard, in Glasgow, to find any sense of elevation. It isn't a castle town, and so, unlike Edinburgh, Stirling, or Inverness, its streets do not curve down from the castle rock. Glasgow was built for a church, by the burn at Molendinar, and its cathedral, medieval, occupies a site used for this purpose since the third century C.E. From the height of the Necropolis beside it, and the Knox Monument at its highest point, it's possible to see the city's skyline, the verdigris roof of

Glasgow Cathedral, and at night, the small halogens that illuminate The Reformer on his podium.

I am a bit uneasy with Knox watching me. I am the son of Irish Catholics, the son of migrants. My grandfather on my father's side was born in Glencoe, where in 1692, thirty-eight MacDonalds were massacred for failing in their loyalty to William of Orange. A strange irony that my grandfather was born there, after his family came from Ireland during the colonisation of the island by the British Crown under James VI. There was also, let us remember, no shortage of Scottish merchants profiting from this new venture. Violence thrums in our veins. There is, nowhere on earth, any bloodline innocent of history. But blood is not something in which we should ever set store; it passes so easily from heart to heart, slips between us careless as a word.

And yet I feel uneasy. The imposing figure of Knox reminds me too much of the great division of Glasgow, a sectarianism which is, when I talk to friends from the Republic and Northern Ireland, simply embarrassing. A civil war reduced to football – Rangers, Celtic, Freemasonry, Orangeism. A diaspora with no sense of struggle, grieving the hurts of the past, while bigots dance to the tune of a tin whistle. This, as much as all that I would praise, is still at the heart of Glasgow.

When I feel Knox's gaze on me, I am reminded of a document published by the Church of Scotland – the Kirk – in 1922: *The Menace of the Irish Race to Our Scottish Nationality*. The Kirk advocated the forced repatriation of the Irish. I wonder if this means that I, too, would have been expelled, thrown back to a country with which I have, at best, the most tenuous of connections, losing as I went the ties that bind me to this place and this people. I am Glasgow on my mother's side for generations, but Irish on my father's. At what point do you stop being a migrant? Is it a matter of years, or of generations? From this vantage, scientific racism seems an impossibility – who could ever endorse that document? But amid the chaos of Brexit, and here, under Knox's gaze, I find it hard to laugh at the Kirk in 1922. History repeats. First as tragedy, then as farce, Marx said. Or history, Stephen tells us in *Ulysses*, is a nightmare from which we are trying to wake.

I was in secondary school the first time someone called me a Fenian. I didn't know what it meant, only that it was intended as an insult. I am from a 'Celtic Family', which means something in Glasgow, but my mum's family was vaguely Protestant, which meant we were never raised in any faith. What faith I have is in society, in people, in connection. My preoccupation with language comes from this, in trying to understand how we connect to each other when we are bound together by something as fragile as a sign. Writing forms a link. But history can be read in many different ways.

Still I find myself on one side, of history and a divide. A side from which it is still possible to be exiled: religion in Scotland has hardly been sympathetic in its approach to gay issues. Even now, there are those 'good Sellick men' who cry martyr for the Catholic in Glasgow. Any stone thrown will hit a number of apologists claiming their religious freedom threatened by the dignity of another. They gather around the issue of faith schools, today. In 2014, it was marriage equality, before that, Section 28. With each issue passed over, a new generation begins to find it hard to believe that such a thing was ever possible. 1922 seems a distant past.

Morgan, in 1999, living, then, as an openly gay man, battled with the Archbishop of Glasgow, Thomas Winning, over Section 28. Winning described homosexuality as a 'perversion', while the *Daily Record*, the paper of Glasgow's Labour, claimed Scottish schoolchildren were receiving 'gay sex lessons' to stoke outrage among the city's working class. So much has changed. But 1922 is not so far from 1999, never so far from today.

Morgan took his revenge on Winning in a poem, 'Section 28', after the bill was repealed. St Peter refuses the Archbishop entry into heaven – the last place has been given to Alan Turing, breaker of the Enigma. A brilliant mind destroyed by the state he had saved: chemical castration, to prevent him acting on his 'perversion'. Turing then took his own life by eating an apple laced with cyanide. Morgan tries to give justice to the dead scientist, who lived between ciphers, finding messages in codes eternally in crisis.

People often wonder why there is such a thing as a queer community. What do they have in common, save for the fact of sex? With men, with women, with the same, or the other. What did Morgan recognise in Turing?

I imagine that for Turing, in his chemical castration, the pain of being was so great it wouldn't have mattered if the apple he ate had been a wooden import from Romania. He would have chewed the splinters and let the ragged *skelfs* tear the truth from his throat as he choked back the night, wanting an end. To it all, to the tension between being and appearance, and the struggle to love in a world he had saved but to which he remained foreign. I think I can understand it, that desire. An end, at last, to exile.

I begin the walk back into the city, trying not to feel, at each step, the shadow of Knox at my back.

*

I have received many language lessons in my life. I remember the collective groans of the class in secondary school when the teacher drew the conjugation table, the chalk on the blackboard screeching along my nerves as she showed us how the verb *parler* had to agree with its subject: *je parle, tu parles, vous parlez, il/elle parle, ils/elles parlent, nous parlons, on parle. Parlez-vous français?* Speak-you French?

The idea of agreement was vague to us. We understood that in English we say 'speaks' in third-person and 'speak' in first. The French system seemed excessive. Then the teacher drew another table, to show us the two forms of the past: *passé composé* and *passé parfait*, and how these too had to agree. Grammatically, by subject, and by gender. The idea was impossible to us. Our brains stopped them at the channel of the ear, refusing the words a visa to enter. They remained were they were. Nonsense. Gobbledegook.

None of this mattered when I learned Japanese. There is no agreement, no declension, no case, and no required subject. It makes up for this with a variety of grammatical nuances and usages that shade meaning, but far more time-consuming is learning the writing system: two forty-eight character syllabaries, and a couple of thousand kanji are required to be functionally literate. I spent countless hours in an apartment in Tokyo writing out ideograph after ideograph after ideograph, trying to cling onto these strange symbols like flotsam in an endless sea.

German, on the other hand, is highly inflected – it has cases, three genders, and requires agreement in all these things, not to mention the way the words get thrown together, prefixes like *ver-* and *ent-* changing the meaning of verbs that seemed familiar. The sentence structure is pliable; verbs fly around, words come apart.

I have had the good fortune to be taught by many brilliant teachers, kind people who opened the world to me, gave Morgan to me, and who put tongues in my head with the patience that requires. I have encountered people, lives, and places that my family before me could never have imagined. For this, I will always be grateful.

But I wasn't raised by these people. They taught me language in tables, and structure, and agreement. They taught me grammar and syntax and how to sound proper. They taught me to be correct in language, something that, for so long, meant so much to me. But these are not the most important lessons I have received.

Like most working-class children, I was raised, in part, by the TV – my early French was learned from a red-haired puppet on a show called *Tots TV*. Both my parents worked, so after school I would go to my gran's, and with her, go to visit Nana Fay and Margaret over in Springburn, where my great-aunt Agnes also lived. We used to walk to the Safeway – bought out by Morrison's now – with me swinging on their arms between them, and on special occasions, I would get a kid's box from the chippy, called Santi's. Then I would sit in front of the TV and watch the shows until my mum came to pick me up after work.

My favourite TV shows were *How 2* and *Alphabet Castle*. (*Knightmare* goes without saying.) These two programmes showed you how the world worked. In

How 2 I learned how to produce water in the desert using five stones and a piece of cling film, and that without smell, food doesn't taste the same: cola, for example, tasted like orange juice. In *Alphabet Castle* they showed me how English worked. They talked about spelling – *wrought, bought, taught*, though this was never explained as a Germanic hangover from Old English – and grammar – *would, should, could* – but my favourite part was always the talking turkey, Gobbledygook. In this part of the programme, a word was shown, scrambled, and it was up to us to unscramble the text and give it meaning. An experience of translation.

Because my parents worked, if I were sick, I'd go to my gran's. If I stayed over, I'd get up early, give the cat a few slices of chicken from the fridge, and watch cartoons in the living room, photos of my granda on a side table, an Artex frieze of a palm tree inexplicably on one wall, and wait until my gran woke up. Then we would watch *This Morning*, where the weatherman jumped on floating islands in the Thames, representing the country we lived in. And then, afterwards, we would watch *Sesame Street* and *Murder, She Wrote*. I always loved seeing Jessica Fletcher on her bike, the idea that her job was to make up stories.

I remember, one day, after we watched our shows, playing with a Franklin Spellmaster, an early computer that helped children with language. We played hangman. My gran taught me the difference between a consonant and a vowel. In conversations between English and Glaswegian, I learned words like *shipwreck, noose*, and *gibbet*. But more importantly, the Spellmaster had a type and speak function, with which my gran taught me words like: *fuck, bastard, arse*, and *fanny*. Between the Spellmaster and my gran's mouth there came two ways of speaking, both of which were forbidden. This, I think, more than any table, was linguistically formative. The language out of frame.

The other lessons are from my mother, who taught me to play with words. In our house we always said a *tiece of post* for a *piece of toast* and *a soul of bereal* for a *bowl of cereal*. We called cheese *queso* and counted in French. She would always shout, 'Come hither tae yer mither.' And teach me to say, 'It's a braw moonlicht nicht the nicht.' Expressions like 'yer ontae plums' and 'lucky white heather' and 'you've won a watch'. *No bother at all* in our house wasn't even *nae bother at aw*, but *nae tother a baw*. Never 'grandad' – always 'granda'.

Of all the lessons I have learned about language

in my life, I think it is these that are most important: the closeness we shared, my gran, my mum, and me (I, I should say, if we're being correct about it), as we took words apart, broke them down, put them together again. A free-playing invention, a different kind of translation. The essence of a *sang*.

*

The bus I am taking into town today, to meet a friend for lunch, travels through Royston, an area with a high population of migrants, refugees, and asylum seekers. Scotland is a country weaning itself off faith. Secularism is outpacing the old gods, but the bus on Sunday is always packed, early in the morning, and always colourful. Women from Africa in their Sunday best, speaking a French which is at once familiar and foreign. I find it strange to think that, despite the distance between Senegal and Glasgow, it is the French language that can connect us. History tangles us together in strange ways. But this is the beauty of a multilingual world, even one which bears the scars of colonialism. A bus in Glasgow, filled with different people, different tongues, different colours, different hearts. Gathered together in one place. There is so much life in this. So much beauty in the fact of movement.

Getting off the bus, I cut across Buchanan Street, down Mitchell Lane, to The Lighthouse. Tucked away like this, it's often overlooked, but one of my favourite places in the city. An old Mackintosh building encased in glass, it is Glasgow's museum of architecture, with a dedicated floor to the architect Charles Mackintosh. But I am not here for the models of his unbuilt buildings, but for a sense of elevation. A touch of clear air that is so hard to find, and harder still, since the destruction of the old Red Road Flats. My mum lived in them, on the fourth floor, for a year. She went from a shared toilet in a tenement to a heated bathroom and a view of the city. An embarrassment, they said, when they were torn down, but they were the height of luxury to the people who moved into them originally. You could see the flats anywhere you went in the east. A distinguishing feature of the city's skyline now nothing but rubble. A new generation will never know what they meant, what dreams they held. As we move forward with the millennium, all the old towers are falling, it seems.

A spiral staircase leads from the Mackintosh exhibit of The Lighthouse to an observation deck up top.

The staircase is narrow, with tourists coming down the other way, or people stopping to take photos on the trudge up or down. And then at the top, a terrace wraps all the way around, showing the Glasgow skyline, with signs to explain its many landmarks: The Royal Concert Hall, The Glasgow School of Art, The City Chambers, The Cathedral, Glasgow University, and the SECC, to the south of the great River Clyde.

There is no mention of the Red Road Flats. The skyline is changed, the city too. It changes, still, every visit. Bars and restaurants come and go. Old and new buildings get reworked as time passes. Nothing stays the same. A part of me fears that these changes are too great; that we are becoming, through the years, strangers to each other. That one day we will have travelled so far from each other, there will be no way back.

Once the doors of a language are opened, it is possible to walk through them and never look back. To leave the past in another room, another life. Many people seek this path, yearning to break free of the trappings of an identity which seem, at times, mutually exclusive. For many years I was trying to escape this feeling by being somewhere else. I am not alone in this. Scotland's problem has never been immigration but emigration.

The world of the mother tongue is a twilight sleep. We sleepwalk through language without knowing its contours, thinking only certain paths are navigable. Our voices flow through given channels and our mouths forget all the variations of sound that are possible. Foreign languages wake us from this slumber. They show us that all the walls we thought confined us were simply doors, waiting to be opened. For me, this door was always slightly ajar.

I have come far from Robroyston, taken many steps since I first counted in French on the couch with my mum. I have opened and walked through many doors in language. But now, rather than finding that I want to keep going, to keep running, I am learning that it is also possible to retrace the steps of language, to open all the locks that once held you back. I think of my mum, and my gran, and all the ways that language shifts between us. Between generations, the code breaks down. But this breaking and resurrection is itself a form of speech. And it is this, now, that I cherish. Far more than being correct. Far more than being posh, grown-up, male, English, and dead.

This spirit of invention is also what I love in

Morgan; the way that, whenever he steps into the past, it is always as a time-traveller. Unlike MacDiarmid, Morgan brings the future into the old language and the old language into the future. In 'The World', he writes: 'Remembrance / offered nothing, swam in our hands. We're here. The past is not our home.' And then, closing the poem, Morgan offers this: 'I don't think it's not being perfect / that brings the sorrows in, but being soon / beyond the force not to be powerless.'

It is difficult not to feel powerless by the way that history moves, in great steps and eras beneath the names of great men. But through this landscape, still, there are the faltering steps of a man trying to catch the bus, the shadows of women falling into water. The lives they might have led. There is failure, and heartbreak, and all the other histories that make us who we are.

I am not the same person I was when I left Glasgow, and Glasgow is not the same city I left. Change, growth, pain; these are the signs of life, of a place that is living. Things must be cleared to make way for the new. The Red Road Flats tumble into ash. From its breaking, a message can always find its resurrection. And even we, when we are broken, must pick up the pieces, the bits of ourselves; what we are and what we were. It is only in these shattered things that we find what might still be.

A deep breath of Glasgow air, the bite of it. I let it fill each dark corner of lung, not just with the sadness of the passing of the past, but a sense of accumulation, momentum, a history that is my own being carried forward. There is in love a great strength, Morgan said, and in 'The Second Life', before he had made his own proclamation of love in the open: 'Many things are unspoken / in the life of a man, and with a place / there is an unspoken love also / in undercurrents, drifting, waiting its time.'

'A great place and its people are not renewed lightly.'

This city has given me lessons in strength, and passion; I have loved and been given love in this city, by people born here, others not, but always by people who have in some way made this place their home. Even when I felt far away, in my own quiet exile – this city and its people have made me welcome.

Across the sky a plane is travelling, bending a long arc through a few frail wisps of cirrus, before once more it begins to rise.

From the windows of that plane, George Square

would appear as a red scrap with a few black dots, one in the centre, slightly larger than the others, while around it yellow cagoules and red windbreakers wheel and spin. La Pasionaria vanishes at a height and the slow trains creep under Venetian glass while lovers kiss and spin beneath the Central clock, saying *I love you I love you* in a hundred tongues. Up, up, over the head of Knox, higher than clouds and all the names of god, till Glasgow itself is simply one piece in a larger pattern, one design in the great tapestry, with two rivers at its heart. The plane goes farther, over Ayrshire, the West Coast, and Arran, over crofts and highland glens, marked by gorse and wild heather, soft scars of forgotten places, people, names, over ruins and cracked castles, the black vastness of the lochs, and island upon island in their water of silver glass.

Between all these places run rivers, motorways, train lines, across distance, diaspora, and death. Threads connecting here with there, and bridges under which history and love have overflowed the boundaries of the centuries. Borders yielding to meltwater, going out, in the dark, with the tide.

From the window of an economy jet, the passengers would see, as they travel elsewhere, all of

A Glasgow Sang

Scotland laid out before them. All the things that it has been, and all the things it might still be. The many threads that gather here, cut and cross and knot here. The strings it binds to the heart here. How they sing.

Acknowledgements

For information on Edwin Morgan's life, I am deeply indebted to James McGonigal's *Beyond the Last Dragon: A Life of Edwin Morgan* (Sandstone Press, 2012). Quotes from Morgan's poetry are taken from my well-worn copy of *New Selected Poems* (Carcanet, 2000), and *A.D.: A Trilogy on the Life of Jesus Christ* (Carcanet, 2000). The poem for the opening of the Scottish Parliament is publically available through the Parliament's website. Translations of Mary MacPherson's songs are modified from those found on www.celticlyricscorner.net, and Lorca's line to La Pasionaria is quoted in her biography, *Memorias de Pasionaria, 1937–1977: me faltaba españa* (Planeta, 1984). I would like to thank everyone at Orion Books involved in Hometown Tales, particularly Jennifer Kerslake and Jade Craddock for their help during the editing process. I would also like to thank Kirsty

Logan and Ryan Vance for being stalwart friends and judicious readers. And lastly, of course, I owe a debt of gratitude to my gran, Gina, and my mother, Alison, who helped me remember all the things I never knew, and who gave me a history to write about. Thank you.

HOMETOWN TALES

AVAILABLE NOW FROM W&N